THE SUPREME LAW OF GRATITUDE
The Ultimate Antidote for Grief

Dr Sylvia Forchap-Likambi

Copyright ©2024 by Dr Sylvia Forchap-Likambi

ISBN 13: 978-1-913266-31-8

All rights reserved. No part of this book may be reproduced or transmitted in any form or by any means, electronic or mechanical, including photocopying, recording, or by an information storage and retrieval system – except by a reviewer who may quote brief passages in a review to be printed in a magazine or newspaper – without permission in writing from the copyright owner.

Other books by the Author:

Visionary Woman: Moved by Purpose, Not by Sight

ISBN-13: 978-1-913266-09-7

Personal & Professional Transformation and Success Planner: Your Blueprint to Success & Abundance in All Areas of Your Life – Parts one and two

ISBN-13: 978-1-913266-08-0

Unleash Your Authentic Identity: Unlock Your True Identity & Purpose

ISBN-13: 978-1-913266-95-0

Success Blueprint: Timeless Principles to Enable You to Identify & Accomplish True Success & Fulfilment in All Areas of Life

ISBN-13: 978-1-913266-98-1

Principles of Resolution: A Practical Step-by-Step Guide to Enable You to Identify, Set & Accomplish Your Goals

ISBN 10: 1543063780

ISBN13:9781543063783

Seven Powerful Strategies for Overcoming Life Challenges: Tested & Proven Life-Changing Keys

ISBN-13: 978-1-913266-02-8

ISBN-10: 1975669584

A Father's Tender and Compassionate Love: A Love so Tender, Compassionate, and Unconditional

ISBN 10: 1479772887/ ISBN 13: 9781479772889

ISBN 10: 1479772879 ISBN/ 13: 9781479772872

DEDICATION

In loving memory of my beloved and darling father, Daddy William Ayuk Forchap, and my cherished mother, Mama Elizabeth Nkem Forchap.

Thank you for the unconditional love, compassion, grace, and care you so generously bestowed upon me. The values and legacy you instilled in me and my siblings continue to live on, shaping our lives even after your departure.

This book is dedicated to you both. It is a profound privilege and honour to write about gratitude, sharing my journey, experiences, and wisdom with a soul as magnificent and extraordinary as yours.

All my love,
Sylvia

ACKNOWLEDGEMENTS

My profound and heartfelt gratitude goes to my darling husband, Pastor Michael Likambi, for your continuous support and love towards me, ensuring that I continue to live a purposeful and fulfilled life and become all that I was created to be.

To my gracious and magnificent children and angels – Latoya, Caleb, and Baby Destiny – for enabling me to experience the exceptional joy and fulfilment that comes with motherhood, I could never have asked for any better! Thank you for making me the incredibly happy and fulfilled mum and role model/ mentor that I am today.

To my beautiful family and wonderful siblings, beloved friends, pastors, staff, colleagues, loved ones, and the millions of men and women I have been privileged to work with and serve globally— thank you for enabling me to fulfil my unique purpose of existence and continue to do so by serving you wholeheartedly with each new day I am blessed and privileged to be alive. Nothing could ever compare to the unique experience and the deep sense of satisfaction and contentment that comes from being truly authentic and living a purposeful life…

Above all, I would like to express endless gratitude and honour to my Heavenly Father and Creator, God, for the magnificent gift of life, purpose, and wisdom! To Him be all the Glory.

Table Of Contents

Preface 1

Chapter 1 – Healthy vs Unhealthy Ways to Grieve 7

Chapter 2 – Cultivating an Attitude of Gratitude 27

Chapter 3 – The Power of Gratitude.. 35

Chapter 4 – Triumphing Over Grief Through Gratitude 51

Chapter 5 – The Role of Perception & Selflessness in Overcoming Grief. 69

Chapter 6 – Decoding The Supreme Law of Gratitude 81

References 131

About the Author 133

About the Publisher 137

Preface

Drawing on personal life stories, experiences of others, divine wisdom, and scientific research, this manuscript explores the transformative power of gratitude as a catalyst for healing and restoration. Through the practice of gratitude, readers are encouraged to shift their focus from what has been lost to what still remains—the blessings, both great and small, that continue to enrich their lives even in times of hardship.

Gratitude is far more than a simple act of kindness or a polite gesture—it has the ability to shape our biological processes, particularly those involving the brain and nervous system. Research highlights that gratitude has a lasting impact on brain function (Zahn et al., 2007), offering a powerful tool for improving mental and physical well-being.

Beyond cultivating self-compassion and empathy, gratitude has been shown to positively affect conditions such as stress, anxiety, and chronic pain.

The *Counting Blessings vs Burdens* study (Emmons & McCullough, 2003) explored how gratitude influences physical health. Participants who regularly maintained a gratitude journal reported a 16% reduction in pain symptoms compared to those who did not. These individuals also demonstrated greater willingness to engage in physical activity and cooperate with treatment. This improvement was linked to the role of gratitude in balancing dopamine levels, enhancing vitality, and reducing the perception of pain.

Gratitude has also been shown to release toxic emotions. The hippocampus and amygdala—key regions of the limbic system responsible for processing emotions—are particularly active when gratitude is expressed, influencing both emotional regulation and memory. A 2018 study by Wong et al. on individuals receiving mental health support found that participants who wrote gratitude letters alongside their therapy sessions showed significant improvements in emotional recovery, while those who wrote about negative experiences reported higher levels of depression and anxiety.

By nurturing positive emotions and rebalancing brain chemistry, gratitude offers a transformative path toward emotional healing and resilience. It reduces mental distress while boosting physical vitality, demonstrating the deep connection between our emotional and physical health.

Gratitude is more than just a momentary emotion or a passing sentiment—it is a way of life, a state of being, and an attitude with which we choose to view and experience the world with renewed optimism and perspective. In cultivating a spirit of gratitude, we are empowered to embrace the fullness of our experiences, finding solace in the beauty that surrounds us even in times of sorrow and distress.

Cultivating and exhibiting an attitude of gratitude is not abstract or as difficult as it's been painted to be in modern times, where our focus has shifted from that of humanity to that of vanity and constant/ increasing expectations and demands on ourselves either by others or by us.

Gratitude has always been a natural way of living when we were children, innocent, and appreciative of life and the little things of life. However, as we grew, our demands, expectations, and desires also grew, resulting in greed and expressions of dissatisfaction and ingratitude. We became almost impossible to satisfy. I perfectly understand that in the face of overwhelming grief, the expression or path to gratitude may seem steep and treacherous, filled with obstacles and setbacks. However, it is in these moments that the true power of gratitude shines brightest, offering an anchor to support and guide us through the storm.

In the pages that follow, we will encounter stories of resilience and recovery—personal stories and experiences, in which, in the depths of despair, I uncovered the transformative power of gratitude that shone through and transformed my life and the lives of countless individuals. From the ashes of loss, we emerged stronger and more resilient, with a heart filled with a profound sense of gratitude for the precious gift of life itself.

As we embark on this journey together, may we approach the exploration of gratitude with open hearts and open minds, ready to embrace the wisdom that lies waiting to be uncovered. For in the power of gratitude, we find not only solace for our sorrow but also the promise of a brighter tomorrow, where hope springs eternal and love knows no bounds.

Hence, let us set forth on this journey with courage and conviction, knowing that in the embrace of gratitude, we find the strength to face even the darkest of days with grace and resilience. For truly, the power of gratitude is the ultimate antidote for grief, offering healing and restoration to all who dare to embrace its transformative power.

The inspiration to write this book and share this profound message stems from my own experiences and those of the hundreds of men and women I have shared this truth with—individuals whose lives have been profoundly transformed. If you are currently grieving as you read this manuscript or have recently lost a loved one or loved ones, I want to share a personal story and experience with you. My sincere hope is that it brings you immense comfort and hope. It is my deepest wish and prayer that it soothes your heart and empowers you to find peace and closure as you navigate your grief.

CHAPTER 1

Healthy vs Unhealthy Ways to Grieve

In this chapter, I will take a few moments to briefly share my personal experience of grief and the power of gratitude in overcoming it, before moving on to the subsequent pages and chapters of this impactful book on gratitude.

Before we proceed further, let us establish a common understanding of what grief is. Grief is defined as deep sadness, especially one caused by the death of someone. It can also relate to profound sorrow brought about by the loss of something dear and significant to us.

Simply put, grief is the experience of great sadness as a result of a loss—whether it be a loved one, a job, a part of our body or health, a relationship, a friendship, a child, or even the life we once dreamed of but never lived. Often, this unfulfilled life is one we feel was taken from us by others or by our own decisions.

In the network of human emotions, grief stands as one of the most profound and universally experienced phenomena. From the raw anguish of loss to the quiet ache of longing, grief encompasses a spectrum of emotions that defy easy categorisation. Yet, within the complex network of grief, lie the seeds of gratitude waiting to take root and flourish.

Grief does not discriminate; it can grip the heart of anyone, irrespective of age, gender, or social status. Grief, with its relentless waves of sorrow, if not dealt with in a healthy and timely manner, has the ability to engulf us in darkness, leaving us feeling lost, depressed, and lonely in a world that suddenly seems unfamiliar and unfair.

Yet, amidst the shadows of sorrow, there exists a light—a beacon of hope that has the power to guide us through even the darkest of times. That light is gratitude. In the subsequent pages, I invite you to embark with me on a journey to explore the transformative power of gratitude as the ultimate and unprescribed antidote for grief.

Of note, gratitude empowers us with the remarkable power and ability to transcend the boundaries of sorrow and illuminate the path to healing. It is a force that, when exercised with intention and sincerity, has the capacity to infuse even the most desolate of scenarios with warmth and vitality.

I, too, have endured the loss of some of the most significant and cherished figures in my life—my parents, my beloved mum and dad and sister. However, for the purpose of this book, I place emphasis on my beloved dad and mum.

Of course, my husband, children, siblings, and extended family are profoundly significant and precious to me as well; I love them profoundly. You, too, are an important part of my life, and I love and value you greatly. Above all, God is the central figure in my life. In Him, I live, in Him, I breathe, and to Him, I owe my being and everything I have, do, and am.

I find solace in knowing that God is always with me, and I choose to focus on His infinite blessings—blessings I neither deserve nor am entitled to. Among these blessings is the incredible privilege of having been gifted the most amazing and loving parents, siblings, and family.

Of note, where our focus goes, our energy flows...

The truth is, when we focus on what we have lost, it becomes lost energy. Because it is already gone and cannot be retrieved, any energy directed towards it is futile. While I may have physically lost my mum, dad, and elder sister, their spirits live on—they are forever in my heart, where they continue to reside. Whenever I express gratitude to God for allowing me to be part of their lives and for bringing them into mine, they come alive within me. I relive the precious and priceless memories I shared with them and find myself filled with gratitude for the blessings they brought into my life. These blessings remain with me to this day.

Though I have lost them physically, they live on within me, and their light continues to shine in my heart and life—and for this, I am eternally grateful. Even as I write these words, I feel my dad's presence during the most significant moments of my life. In times when I must make crucial, life-changing decisions, dad is always with me. They are ever-present in my heart. When I focus on this profound truth, my perspective shifts, and this dynamic brings renewed life into my soul.

I feel them come alive again. I know they are watching over me, and I imagine them saying: "My beloved daughter, 'Mama' and 'Samba Little'"—as Dad and Mum fondly called me—"I'm so proud of you. I'm proud of the woman you've become, proud of the work you are doing, and proud of the light you are shining in the lives of others. I am with you throughout this journey, smiling with you because I am profoundly honoured to have been your dad/mum."

Mum would undoubtedly add: "I am proud that you have embraced the powerful gift of prayer that I held so dear. I have never left your life; I am always with you."

However, if I were to focus on their physical absence and the sense of loss, my energy would be unproductive. It would be directed towards something irretrievably lost, something that cannot be brought back to life. Such energy would be unrecoverable, leaving me drained, depleted, and even prone to despair. By contrast, focusing on the life within me replenishes my energy and fills me with vitality. It brings more life, revives my spirit, and empowers me to feel fortified and truly alive.

Energy, as we know, is neither created nor destroyed—it is transformed from one state to another: from death to life, sadness to joy, resentment to forgiveness, anger to peace, hatred to love, and so on.

Having briefly shared my experience of grief, which I will explore in greater detail later, I would now like to invite you to join me in channelling your focus and energy towards gratitude and life. We are privileged to be alive today and to embrace the gift of the present moment—a precious treasure to be cherished and valued. We cannot afford to dwell on the past or linger in its shadows.

Yes, you might have lost your loved one(s), your job, or even your health. What is the ideal experience you would like to create today that is healthy and aligns with your purpose—allowing you to experience a sense of inner peace and harmony? Write down your answers and reflect on them, shifting your focus and energy to what you want to create and experience. Remember, you and I are responsible for creating our realities.

I invite you once again to join me as we express gratitude. What do you have to be grateful for today? When you focus on gratitude, you'll find that you become happier and experience more peace. Your soul aligns with your spirit, bringing harmony within.

Knowing what you know now, would you choose gratitude over grief today? Would you choose gratitude over death? Would you count your blessings rather than your losses?

Write down all the things and people in your life that you are most grateful for, especially those that could never be replaced by money.

Say to yourself:

> *"I choose to express gratitude today and not make excuses for my life. I choose to embrace life and good health, and not to justify any feelings that are destructive to my well-being. I choose to allow myself to receive and experience the gift of this day—a gift I do not deserve yet have been given. I choose to walk through this day in gratitude, being cheerful and thankful as I step into my future. I am profoundly grateful to be alive today."*

In the spirit of gratitude, I must confess that I am eternally thankful for the unique privilege and honour of serving you. I am grateful for the opportunity to share this moment with you and to recount my journey of living life fully—losing, and yet, gaining. Although I lost my parents, I gained their love—unconditional love and light that remain with me and within me. I am grateful for every second of my life and for the blessing of being alive.

I often hear people say things like, *"It's okay to grieve for as long as you need to... People grieve differently... Let's be empathetic and accommodating."* While this is true, I encourage you to develop a deeper understanding of the significant role our perception of life, death, loss, and grief plays in shaping our experiences and realities. Our perceptions of what we have lost—or what we are grateful for—and the meanings and narratives we attach to them ultimately create our lived realities, including how we experience grief.

Two people could lose the exact same loved one—a parent or another significant figure—and yet grieve in entirely different, even contradictory ways. This demonstrates that grief isn't solely about the loss itself. Instead, it has everything to do with us—who we are and how we perceive death, loss, and the people we have lost. Every explanation or reason we give for our grief can often be summed up as "excuses" or "justifications." Please forgive me if these terms sound harsh. However, they represent the rationales we offer to ourselves and others to feel more comfortable, understood, or validated in our current situation, state of grief, or depression.

Let me share this with you, my beloved: we are not born to justify every action or reaction. We don't need to explain ourselves when we are living in truth and authenticity. Being truthful and authentic with ourselves is enough. We don't need to convince anyone. The deep inner peace and serenity we experience in such moments are indicators of alignment with our true selves and harmony with the divine purpose for our lives.

On the contrary, when we grieve in an unhealthy manner, we don't experience a sense of deep inner peace—we constantly feel the loss, void, anger, and resentment. This state is not in alignment with our being. It is not the way we were designed to function, and as a result, there is no peace or closure. Instead, we experience unrest, and our health is negatively affected. This is unhealthy.

While I cannot tell you how to grieve or how not to grieve—since there is no definitive right or wrong way, and I certainly do not consider myself qualified to dictate such things—I can, however, tell you this: there is a healthy way to grieve and an unhealthy way to grieve. Everything unhealthy ultimately harms us, as it is not in alignment with how we are designed to function. It begins to negatively affect our health and well-being.

It's similar to why I cannot tell you how to eat or how not to eat, but I can certainly tell you that some foods are healthy while others are unhealthy. Furthermore, when we eat something unhealthy—or eat in an unhealthy way—no matter how much we try to justify it, if it doesn't work to improve our health or enable us to thrive in optimal health, then it is unhealthy. It is damaging and detrimental to our well-being.

Conversely, when we eat healthily, the benefits are enormous. In much the same way, when we grieve in a healthy manner, the benefits are profound. This was exactly my experience when I lost my mum and dad.

I hereby share with you a real-life story depicting healthy vs. unhealthy ways to grieve. Here is the story of Jane:

Jane, a 45-year-old woman from Liverpool, was devastated when she lost her mother after a long battle with cancer. Her mother had been her best friend, confidante, and pillar of support, and the thought of life without her seemed unbearable. Jane's grieving process, however, soon became an example of the stark contrast between healthy and unhealthy ways to cope with loss.

Unhealthy Grieving:

Initially, Jane's grief was all-consuming. For weeks after her mother's passing, she could hardly get out of bed. She refused to leave her house, not wanting to face the outside world. She avoided speaking to friends and family, feeling as though no one could understand her pain. She would often replay in her mind the final moments of her mother's life, obsessively going over every conversation they had, wondering if she had done enough for her.

Her physical health began to decline. She stopped eating, lost a significant amount of weight, and struggled with insomnia. Jane often found herself crying uncontrollably or becoming irritable at the smallest things. She withdrew into herself, consumed by feelings of anger and bitterness. She found it difficult to accept that her mother was truly gone, and she clung to memories, refusing to let go.

This way of grieving was unhealthy because it kept Jane stuck in the past. She found herself unable to process her emotions in a constructive way, holding onto her pain rather than finding a way to move through it. Her lack of self-care and refusal to seek support from others only deepened her sense of isolation.

A Turning Point - Discovering Healthy Grieving:

One day, Jane attended a support group for people who had lost loved ones. It was there that she met Mary, a woman who had experienced a similar loss. Mary's attitude was strikingly different. While she also mourned her mother, she had been making a conscious effort to focus on self-care and personal growth. She told Jane that although grieving was necessary, it was important to also honour the life that had been lived and the positive impact that person had on her life.

Mary shared that after the initial shock of her loss, she had started going for daily walks to clear her mind, had resumed attending yoga classes, and had made a point of maintaining connections with her family and friends. She explained that she had allowed herself to feel sadness, but also made room for moments of joy and gratitude for the time she had spent with her mother.

Inspired by Mary's approach, Jane started to make small but significant changes in her own life. She began to recognise the importance of grieving but realised she had to do so in a way that allowed her to heal, not stay stuck. She reached out to a therapist to help her process her grief and started keeping a gratitude journal. Writing allowed her to express her feelings without feeling judged, and through the practice of gratitude, she started to gain a sense of peace.

She also took up running, something her mother had always encouraged her to do for its physical and mental health benefits. Although it was difficult at first, she found solace in the rhythm of her footsteps and the quiet time to reflect on her mother's legacy. With time, Jane learned to balance her grief with gratitude for the life her mother had given her, choosing to remember the happy moments rather than focusing solely on the loss.

Over the course of several months, Jane began to emerge from her grief in a much healthier way. She still missed her mother deeply, but she had made peace with the reality of her loss. Jane now understood that grieving was not about staying in a state of constant sorrow, but rather about honouring the memory of her loved one while also embracing and being grateful for the life she still had.

She began to rebuild her emotional and physical health, seeking out support when needed and engaging in activities that nourished her soul. Jane's story is a powerful reminder that while grief is inevitable and necessary, how we choose to navigate it makes all the difference. Healthy grieving is about acknowledging the pain but also expressing gratitude for the life lived, while taking steps towards healing, self-care, and personal growth.

By shifting her perspective and adopting healthy grieving practices, Jane was able to transform her sorrow into strength, allowing her to move forward with hope, gratitude, and a renewed sense of purpose.

Key Lesson and Takeaway:

Jane's journey illustrates the contrast between unhealthy and healthy grieving. Unhealthy grieving can keep us stuck in the past, leading to physical and emotional decline, while healthy grieving allows us to mourn the loss while still embracing life. Seeking support, taking care of oneself, and finding moments of gratitude can help us navigate grief in a way that honours our loved ones without losing ourselves in the process.

At the depths of my grief, I found myself reflecting and asking some honest and profoundly important questions. I wondered: *Would I rather God had taken me instead of my parents?* No parent would ever want their child to die before them or in their place. Why, then, was I holding on to what I believed I was entitled to, refusing to embrace the gift and blessings of today and this moment?

I reflected further: *My mum and dad have gone to rest. I wasn't entitled to them—God blessed me with them for a unique purpose: so they could be my mother and father, giving me the gift of life. This allowed me the privilege to exist and to fulfil my own God-given purpose.*

The deeper I sank into the pit of grief and sorrow, the more I reflected. I thought to myself: *How dare I hold on to their passing? They came into my life for a purpose—to bring me into existence so that I might have life and live it to the fullest. Their purpose, among others, was to nurture, nourish, and guide me so that I might fulfil my own purpose in life. Now God has taken them, and here I am focusing on their loss when I should be focusing on the life they gave me. How ungrateful am I?*

God used them as channels to give me life. Now that their lives have been taken, I continue to live because they chose not to abort me, because they chose to come together in that predestined moment so that I could be conceived and brought into the world. Yet here I am, alive, consumed by sorrow and grief—making excuses and justifying my pain every single day that I am here without them. *How is this helpful?*

After all this reflection, questioning, and deep soul-searching, I came to the awareness and understanding that I embody the love of my mum and dad. Their love lives within me—in my heart, a place beyond the physical body, where only love and gratitude reside. I made the decision to carry their light with me, letting it shine in my life to this day.

I chose to be grateful to God. Although my mum, dad, one of my sisters, and other dear relatives have passed, God has kept me alive so that I might, perhaps, write this book, share this powerful message with you, and fulfil one of the many purposes of my existence. I am truly grateful. He gives, and He takes away; who am I to question Him?

When He gives, I am grateful, I receive, and I am thankful. Yet, when He takes away, I cling to what has been taken, unwilling to open my heart and hands to receive what He is pouring out to me today—because my focus remains fixed on yesterday, years ago, or on what I have lost.

I hereby invite you to join me in cultivating a lifestyle of gratitude and healthy living, regardless of what you are going through. A grateful heart is a cheerful heart and undoubtedly serves as medicine for the soul.

Make gratitude your way of life, and you will find yourself grieving healthily, just as I did and as so many others are doing.

Seven Practical and Healthy Ways to Grieve and Their Benefits

1. Acknowledge Your Emotions

Allow yourself to feel a full range of emotions—sadness, anger, guilt, and even moments of relief or joy when you recall fond memories. Journaling or simply sitting in quiet reflection can help process these feelings.

Benefit: Suppressing emotions can lead to mental and physical health problems. Acknowledging them helps you process your grief in a natural, healthy way and reduces the risk of emotional burnout.

2. Seek Strength from God and the Support of Others

Deepen your connection with God and your spiritual life while also reaching out to trusted friends, family members, or a support group. Relying on God for strength, comfort, and healing, combined with sharing your feelings, can provide relief and foster a sense of belonging and hope.

Benefit: Talking about your loss helps release pent-up emotions, while reliance on God and support from others reminds you that you are not alone in your journey. This approach offers both spiritual and emotional solace.

3. Practise Gratitude

Focus on the blessings in your life. Write down a minimum of three things you're thankful for each day, even if they are small.

Benefit: Gratitude shifts your perspective from loss to abundance, promoting a sense of hope and resilience while reducing feelings of helplessness.

4. Transform Your Pain to a Bigger Purpose

Channel your grief into meaningful work or a cause that resonates with you—such as starting a foundation in your loved one's name, volunteering, or supporting others who are grieving.

Benefit: Turning pain into purpose gives your grief a constructive outlet, creating a legacy that honours your loved one while fostering a sense of fulfilment and empowerment.

5. Engage in Physical Activity

Incorporate gentle exercises like walking, dancing, or swimming into your routine. Exercise outdoors if possible, to benefit from fresh air and nature.

Benefit: Physical activity releases endorphins, which improve mood and reduce feelings of stress or depression. Movement also provides a sense of routine and stability.

6. Create a Memory Box or Tribute

Collect meaningful items—photos, letters, or souvenirs—that remind you of your loved one. Dedicate a special place for these items or create a tribute book.

Benefit: Memorialising your loved one allows you to cherish their memory in a positive way, helping to turn your grief into gratitude for the moments you shared.

7. Talk to a Therapist or Counsellor

Seek professional help to work through complex emotions, especially if your grief feels overwhelming or prolonged.

Benefit: A therapist can provide coping strategies tailored to your unique needs. They offer a safe, non-judgmental space to explore your feelings, helping you gain insight and clarity.

Unique Benefits of These Strategies

Emotional Balance: Healthy grieving techniques reduce feelings of being overwhelmed and encourage emotional regulation.

Spiritual Resilience: Turning to God for strength provides comfort, meaning, and a renewed sense of faith during difficult times.

Physical Well-being: Activities like exercise help maintain overall health, counteracting the fatigue and lethargy that often accompany grief.

Improved Relationships: Sharing grief with loved ones fosters closeness and mutual understanding, strengthening your support network.

Lasting Memories: Creating a tribute ensures your loved one's memory is honoured in a meaningful and eternal way.

Increased Hope: Gratitude practices and therapy instil optimism and a forward-looking mindset.

Empowered Purpose: Transforming pain into purpose provides a sense of accomplishment and helps turn grief into a force for good.

Holistic Healing: Combining emotional, physical, spiritual, and social approaches to grieving promotes comprehensive well-being and recovery.

By embracing these strategies, you can navigate grief in a healthy way that honours your loved one, nurtures your well-being, and fosters a life filled with hope and purpose.

CHAPTER 2

Cultivating an Attitude of Gratitude

"Never let a day go by without looking for at least one thing in your life to be happy and grateful for...there will be hundreds of reasons to be grateful, if your focus is on finding them."
Dr Sylvia Forchap-Likambi

As you read these words and reflect on this chapter, I invite you to take a moment to pause. Look around you, look within yourself, and reflect on your life. Write down the things you are most grateful for today. Aim to identify at least ten blessings—things money cannot buy.

These might include your health, the gift of being alive, or the relationships you cherish—starting with your relationship with yourself, and then with your loved ones: your spouse (if you have one), your children (if you have children), and your wider family and friends.

Let me guide you by sharing some examples from my own life—things I am profoundly grateful for that no amount of money could ever purchase:

- The gift of life: To wake up this morning and experience the gift of life is a privilege for which I am deeply thankful.

- My health and well-being: I am eternally grateful for the blessing of good health and the well-being that sustains me each day.

- Relationships with myself, my husband, my children, and my family: These relationships are invaluable—and I am eternally grateful for them. They are uniquely cherished and profoundly enrich my life.

- My relationship with you: This connection with you, dear reader, is a gift that money cannot buy. It is an extraordinary privilege to be invited into your personal space—your thoughts, your heart—through the words of this book. Whether I speak to you for a few moments, an hour, a week, or a year, I am deeply grateful. I do not take your time, trust, or presence for granted.

You are under no obligation to listen to me or to read this book. You might even wonder, "Who are you, and why should I pay attention to what you write?" Yet, here you are, sharing this moment with me. For this incredible honour and privilege, I sincerely thank you.

As the saying goes, "Gratitude could turn a meal into a feast, a house into a home, a friend into family, and death into life."

Now, I encourage you to take a moment for yourself. Reflect on the blessings in your own life. Think of at least three things you are most grateful for today—things that no money could ever purchase. Write them down below.

Your journey into gratitude starts with this simple yet profound exercise. May it open your heart to the beauty and abundance in your life.

TODAY I AM MOST GRATEFUL FOR:

....
....
....
....
....
....
....

I love expressing gratitude daily because it is a powerful way of life—an incredibly transformative attribute that enriches our existence. Gratitude is a trait we must consciously incorporate into our daily lives if we truly wish to live fully and thrive.

Be happy, be cheerful, be joyful, and most importantly, be grateful. Gratitude is vital because it shifts our focus away from what we lack or long for, redirecting it towards the abundance we already possess. When we consciously reflect on what we are most grateful for, we remove our attention from scarcity and loss, and instead, celebrate our blessings.

When our focus lingers on what we have lost, what we do not have, or what is absent from our lives, we open ourselves to grief and longing. Remember this simple truth: *where our focus goes, our energy flows*. Why then would we choose to focus on what we no longer have?

Why would I allow myself to dwell on something I lost yesterday, ten days ago, or even years ago, when today—this brand-new and blessed day—has arrived, filled with gifts, opportunities, and privileges I do not deserve yet have been graciously given? Today, the present moment, is a treasure—a gift overflowing with endless possibilities.

Why, then, choose to pour my energy into mourning what is gone when I could instead direct it towards celebrating the life I have right now?

Some of us carry the burdens of loss for years, perhaps even decades. Yet, to do so is to neglect the beauty of the present. How ungrateful I would be to behave in such a manner. I speak from personal reflection, not to pass judgement on others. When we focus solely on everything we have lost, while failing to cherish the privileged lives we have today, we are indeed being ungrateful.

This truth applies universally: to live in gratitude is to honour the blessings of the present, while letting go of the weight of the past. It is only in this act of letting go that we can embrace the fullness of today and thrive in the abundance that life continually offers us.

This is why I asked you at the beginning of this chapter to count your blessings and be grateful for them; to shift your focus to what you are most grateful for that money cannot purchase. Think about these:

Do I deserve to breathe this free air I'm breathing today? Have I earned it? No.

Do I deserve to drink the water I am drinking today? Have I earned it? No.

Do I deserve to receive the unconditional love of God that I am receiving today and every other day? Have I earned it? No.

Do I deserve to have the "unconditional" and maybe sometimes, "conditional" love of my husband that I'm having today? Have I earned it? No.

Do I deserve to thrive in optimal health and wellbeing as I am thriving today? Have I earned it? No. I know I do my very best to keep fit and stay healthy, I also eat and drink healthily, but is this a definite guarantee or passport to infinite health and wellbeing? No.

Some people live the healthiest lives we could ever experience physically, but yet, are struck by a mysterious plaque or sudden illness or heart attack. We have seen "supposedly" healthy and fit footballers with no past history of ill health, suddenly collapse on the field and die. Some people eat the healthiest stuff that I do not even eat and they exercise day and night, yet, they are dead today. It's a privilege and honour to be healthy and alive, and I'm grateful because I do not deserve it– the gifts of life and health have been freely given to me.

Gratitude is a powerful and very fulfilling attitude and life experience. The more grateful you are in life, the more fulfilled/satisfied and happy you are with your life and the surrounding circumstances. This is so because "the feel good hormones" are released and you tend to focus on the things you already possess or are sure of possessing, which implies your focus is not on what you don't have, have lost, or need, but rather it is on what you already have or you are certain you will have. When you do this very often, there is no room for wanting, regret, ingratitude, grief, or worry. On the contrary, you constantly find yourself in a position of satisfaction, abundance, acknowledgement, and appreciation of life—regardless of other obvious challenges or obstacles you may be facing in life.

CHAPTER 3

The Power of Gratitude

"Gratitude unlocks the fullness of life. It turns what we have into enough, and more. It turns denial into acceptance, chaos to order, confusion to clarity. It can turn a meal into a feast, a house into a home, a stranger into a friend. Gratitude makes sense of our past, brings peace for today and creates a vision for tomorrow."
Melody Beattie

"A cheerful heart is good medicine, but a broken spirit saps a person's strength." Proverbs 17:22

In this chapter, we would unlock the miraculous power of gratitude and its ability to:

- *unlock the fullness of life*
- *turn what we have into enough, and more.*

- *transform denial into acceptance,*
- *transform chaos to order,*
- *transform confusion to clarity.*
- *transform a meal into a feast,*
- *transform a house into a home,*
- *turn a stranger into a friend.*
- *make sense of our past,*
- *bring peace for today*
- *create a vision for tomorrow.*

Consequently, as you experience loss and grief of any kind and continue towards your journey of gradually overcoming grief or the challenges and adversities you are faced with, it is fundamental and highly therapeutic that you exhibit an attitude of gratitude. Be grateful for the gift of life, be grateful for the opportunity presented to you for change; be grateful for each new day; be grateful for each step encountered and overcome—even for the ones still to be encountered and overcome. Be thankful for the fact that you are still alive—for good health … as some might not have survived the situation you are currently going through, while others' health might have completely deteriorated if faced with a similar situation or challenge.

THE SUPREME LAW OF GRATITUDE

"Be thankful for what you have; you'll end up having more. If you concentrate on what you don't have, you will never, ever have enough." Oprah Winfrey

Be thankful at all times, regardless of what the situation might be. At the very least, it is not over yet and you are given another chance to make it right again—maybe two, three, four, or five more chances ... you may never know. As long as you are alive, then there is still hope for you—the battle is not over yet, and you are not a victim but a victor. Be thankful for the fact that the current situation or your grief has not consumed and drowned you—you are still swimming in the ocean of adversity and grief. Yes, you are, surely and steadily, to the shore of life, rest, and resolution—still sane, or half sane, and free.

On the other hand, has your grief resulted in a health challenge? Is your mental health affected? Whatever it may be, no one is undermining it and neither should you undermine it, nor have to justify to anyone why you feel the way you do about the situation. Your feelings/emotions, perceptions, and thoughts are valid— whatever they may be.

At the least, you are not locked up in some sort of a prison or psychiatric ward (even if you are, you are still alive, and therefore there is hope for you too). Change is still possible—it is the only thing in life that is constant and guaranteed and happens all the time by the seconds, minutes, hours, days, weeks, months, and years.

Therefore, if you are reading this book while you or a loved one of yours is currently in prison or in a psychiatric home, do not be discouraged or give up just yet—there is still immense hope for you and/or your loved one. Be thankful for the priceless gift of life itself—for where there is life there is also hope. Only the living can have hope. Again, be thankful for another unique opportunity to settle scores and make it right again.

I will tell you about an incident that happened to me a while ago and how consciously adopting and implementing an attitude of gratitude greatly transformed the entire situation and made it an experience worth living/very fulfilling and productive—amidst the challenges that preceded the circumstances.

Five years ago, we had booked a return journey to Dublin, Ireland, for a family vacation. We were supposed to travel by air very early in the morning for our outbound journey (which was a 55-minute journey) so we would have enough time to pick up our hired car, drive to our hotel, check in, explore the city, and rest. Unfortunately, due to some unforeseen circumstances and inappropriate planning, we finally arrived at our departure gate a minute after the final boarding call was made ... only to be told our plane was ready for take-off and the gate was now closed—so they could no longer board us! We were absolutely devastated! If you have ever travelled with three young children, including a one-year-old baby then you will understand the logistics involved when travelling with young ones by air! It had been a long and stressful process from arrival to check-in/security checks, etc. only to finally arrive at the gate to be told we had missed our flight and couldn't travel!

My husband and I were so upset, while our daughter and son thought it was funny—that is the beauty and innocence of children. We were then told we would have to take the next flight, which was due in four hours, and were escorted by the security team through another route to the main departure terminal for a complete start over again!

My husband (whose default position is always to blame me for any lateness) immediately entered into his default position, in spite of all that I had been doing/done to facilitate our early departure and arrival! To my astonishment, he immediately kick-started his default blame mood, which I couldn't really bear or take in. As a result, and out of frustration, I also lashed out, refusing to take the blame and pointing out very firmly that it was a joint responsibility—and if we had planned properly, collaborated, and worked as a team, then the end result would have been completely different. We would never have missed the flight nor arrived late at the airport to start with. But being who he is – with a very strong conviction about his opinions – he wouldn't admit anything different, let alone take responsibility for having contributed to the incident. He even lashed out at the kids as well, blaming them for the delay and incidence! To me, this was absolutely wrong and unacceptable as it is our key responsibility as parents to ensure they wake up on time and be on time. As much as we must train them to become responsible, yet, we cannot blame them for a collective action we needed to take to ensure things were intact.

Our differences in opinion, coupled with our disappointment and frustrations, led to a heated argument, which was absolutely uncalled for! At one point I had to decisively and quickly take the opportunity to focus on the first powerful strategy outlined in this book (reflection and silence) to help me overcome the challenging situation I was then faced with. I immediately and consciously decided to channel my energy and focus within rather than outward and reflect on the situation, but with a focus on the solution rather than the problem itself.

While I reflected, my husband immediately said we were no longer travelling and had to return home—so this could serve as a life lesson to us all, excluding him, of course! I tried to explain to him as calmly as possible about the implications and great financial loss we would incur for making such a negative and emotional decision.

Now back at the departure desk, I went on to enquire about the time and cost of the next flight to Dublin. To my greatest surprise and disappointment, the flight that was due in four hours was fully booked, making it practically impossible for us to depart within the next four hours. The only option given to us was to wait for the subsequent flight, which still had some availability and was due in 11 hours! I stood there astounded yet determined not to give up but to find a solution. Now, with a solution-focused mindset, I suddenly remembered that it was possible to also travel to Dublin via the train/ferry line—and this created a spark of hope and determination again within me.

I was then ushered to the information desk, where I could get all the relevant information I needed to go Dublin from Liverpool on the same day. In all this, I deliberately decided not to approach my husband (who was apparently waiting for me to join him so we could go back home) and to avoid any sort of futile and unproductive communication with him. I was determined to change my perception about the entire incident and remain optimistic. I was not ready for any cynical comments or pessimism as these would have been quite draining and discouraging.

To cut a long story short, I decided to make a very deliberate and conscious decision—that, irrespective of all the ups and downs, I was going to remain grateful and focus on all the reasons and things I had to be grateful for—and there were quite a lot! I started off expressing gratitude for being alive and having amazing health then for having a second chance to make it right—for another opportunity to still travel to Dublin earlier on that same day.

Everything was eventually sorted out, and we were scheduled to take the next train from Liverpool within an hour from then, so we were able to board the ferry to Dublin, which was due to depart within the next five hours. While on the train and ferry, I had much time to ponder and reflect again on all the amazing things and opportunities I should be grateful for.

Finally, on arrival at Dublin, I was so grateful for journey mercies and for the beautiful scenery. I was very grateful that we had finally made it in the end and did not lose everything. I was grateful for the awesome and fabulous quality family time away from every other distraction. In effect, I decided that I was going to make it the best vacation in my life so far! In fact, I became so self-aware and conscious that every moment of my vacation was centred on gratitude and making the best of it. I immediately stopped talking about the past… and began living in the moment and enjoying every single moment the best I could.

I spent a considerable amount of time also reflecting on my life and how I could consistently work on developing myself and living and enjoying life to the fullest—with no regrets whatsoever! At the end of the vacation, I was greatly refreshed, re-energised and restored! Indeed, it was one of my best and quality vacations ever.

In the second part of this chapter, I would like to share with you another story that uncovers the miraculous power entrapped in gratitude. This happened nine years ago, when I was planning to launch one of my new ventures. There was a lot of pressure on my team and me to get everything sorted and ready on time so as to meet the deadline of the launch. Part of the main problem that held us back was the fact that we did not gain access to our new premises on the expected and scheduled date, due to some delays on the part of the previous tenants. This delay caused us huge setbacks with regards to the timescale allocated for refurbishment and decoration of the premises prior to the launch. No one was available to execute the work within 48 hours of the launch at such short notice.

Even though we were amateurs when it came to painting/decoration work, we collectively agreed as a team to take up the task, in addition to other workloads we had. In the course of initiating the work, I realised we were doing more damage than good and making the venue look more unattractive than it was prior to the start of our work. At this, I hesitantly told my colleague who was the lead, and determined to learn as we progressed (and who was by now very stressed and almost covered with paint), that I was profoundly grateful for his commitment and dedication but I didn't think this was a good idea. I told him it would be a good idea to stop the work, clean ourselves up, and the room we were currently painting, and try to get a professional to do the job.

He was not very happy with this decision and became even more stressed. His temperament and body language were not very helpful at a time like this. In all honesty and sincerity, I thanked him for his loyalty and dedication and assured him I fully understood how stressful and urgent the situation was and that I took full responsibility for this and I was doing everything possible to make it right and less stressful for the team—in the best possible way I could. I went further to tell him that, at this point in time, we needed more positive energy and strength than ever before and this could only stem from within us.

On the other hand, I got him to understand that being in a negative and pessimistic mood and environment was futile and detrimental. I then assured him that it was ok for him to take a break and go home to rest and unwind and be back the next day. At that point in time, I did not need any form of negativity around me, especially as I had only just recently found out that I was about 10 weeks pregnant with my third child! I was somehow physically frail and suffering from morning sickness and needed to preserve every form of positive energy I possibly could to keep me mentally, emotionally, and physically strong and fit.

I also reminded my colleague that just as positivity is contagious, so too is negativity—and, even worse, as it saps the energy out of us. We then carried on to clean and tidy up the mess we had made. I kept singing songs of praise and thanksgiving, and being especially thankful for everything that had gone well so far, as I continued to work. I was thankful for the premises, thankful for the new venture, for the amazing and supportive staff I had, and above all for the grace and gift of optimism, serenity, and tenacity—amidst all odds. This attitude of mine gave me a deep sense of reassurance and confidence that everything would be fine.

In the meantime, I browsed through my contacts in search of any builder or painter I could get hold of at such short notice. While I did this, one of my colleagues and the caterer for the launch walked into the building to do some decoration work in the area where she was going to be serving the buffet. I realised that she had also come in with some paint and I asked her if she could paint. Immediately she told me no but that her uncle, who was behind her, was a professional painter and was going to help her!

Another light bulb moment! I lit up with a very bright smile and joy within me and immediately turned to her uncle and asked with a massive smile on my face, "Could you please help us do some decoration work here? We are stuck and almost stranded. Please," I continued with an even brighter smile this time. "Could you help us, please? We need it done within 48 hours!" I added.

He smiled at me and said, "Yes I can. Show me around, so I can see all the work that needs to be done," he added.

By now, I was screaming and jumping like a toddler who had just been given his favourite toy and saying, "Thank you! Thank you! Thank you very much!" We then discussed the costs, and it was a pretty good offer too! That was one problem out of the way, and I was forever so grateful and optimistic. Besides, my colleague was now smiling as well…

The next problem we had was getting our service brochure printed and delivered to us on time for the launch! There had been some major incompatibility problems with our original design that was sent for print in respect to the printing specifications and guidelines. Our designer was not immediately available to resolve this problem when it was first identified and brought to our attention. This meant that we incurred further delays. However, when the designer became available, he immediately got in touch with the printing agency staff and started liaising with them to get the brochure in the correct format requested. They copied me in on all email correspondence and were very committed to resolving the problem at hand. I just couldn't stop thanking both of them for the relentless effort they were all putting in to get this sorted in time.

Each time I had the opportunity to speak with anyone of them, I would say thank you. Notably, the lady at the printing agency kept on saying to me, "You do not have to thank me, I have not done anything … and, besides, I am simply doing my job."

Yet, I wouldn't stop thanking her and her colleagues for everything they had done so far. I told her, "Besides effectively communicating with us at each stage of the project, you have been liaising with our designer to ensure everything is ok and gets to you on time—something you are not obliged to do as it wasn't a part of your service to us … and for this, I am truly grateful."

On another occasion, when I expressed gratitude towards her and her team, she said, "We haven't done anything…"

I said, "Yes, you have done a lot, and whatever the outcome is – even if we do not manage to get the reviewed brochure to you on time to be printed for the launch – I am still very grateful for your service and support towards us." I kept assuring her that she had done so much to get us to this stage and that, regardless of what happened, we would be forever grateful for this act of kindness and empathy she and her team had shown towards us, irrespective of whether we got the leaflets in time for the launch or not.

After an hour or so, she sent me an email informing me that she would be going home at 5:30 p.m. but she would ensure that someone was in the office to hand over the brochures to me when they were done. Not knowing what to do or say anymore, I just kept saying, "Thank you, thank you, thank you… I am profoundly grateful." She then sent me another email, after having just spoken to me on the phone, saying that she just wanted to inform me that she was off now and leaving the office but had arranged for her colleague (whose name and contact number she also included in the email) to hand over the brochures to me on my arrival. I thanked her again for the great work. Then she added that her colleague was going to call me when the brochures were ready.

As I got ready to leave the office that evening, I received a phone call from a local number, which I immediately presumed was coming from their office. To my amazement, it was my local television studio calling to enquire if they could come and cover the launch of our new venture, which was a new health and well-being clinic. The journalist told me that they found the vision and objectives very timely and inspiring and believed it was a project worth sharing with the people of Liverpool. I was speechless and astonished by how quickly and effortlessly all this happened. Usually, I would have had to make several calls accompanied by emails to a handful of media/TV outlets in an effort to get them interested in our projects and events. Here I was, without a single email or call made, and the local TV was looking for us to broadcast our launch! In fact, I immediately accepted without giving it a second thought—and, of course, expressed gratitude to them! I kept on singing songs of thanksgiving as I prepared to leave the office that evening.

It was about 6:00 p.m. when I finally left the office and made my way to my car. As I got into my car, I received another phone call from the printing agency. This time, I was told that everything was ready and they were waiting for me to come and collect the brochures. I trusted the company and everything was perfectly packaged and handed to me on my arrival. I was profoundly humbled and grateful for their kindness towards me and my team. In fact, the brochures were flawless and spot on. The launch was a huge success and indeed one of our best launches ever—with very little effort on our part.

Now, why am I telling you all these stories? The reason behind these stories is to encourage and challenge you to practice gratitude in every given situation and/or storm in life and at all times—by sharing with you some personal real-life examples where the amazing power of gratitude was experienced in its most authentic and transformational form. Gratitude is a very rewarding and fulfilling/ healthy lifestyle and choice. Whenever you show gratitude to those around you, they simply want to do more and may sometimes even go out of their way to support and encourage you with a joyful heart.

Gratitude instantly changes the dynamics of things and your circumstances and produces a sensation of assurance, fulfilment, and tranquillity. Furthermore, it has the power to unlock numerous doors of endless opportunities and favour available to you! It is absolutely and inevitably the ultimate garment and perfume to wear each time you step out of bed and your home! Never put a limit on the number of times you say thank you in a day. Let your ability to say thank you be bountiful and overflowing all day long…

I have literally observed and experienced the power of gratitude work miracles both in the lives of close friends and loved ones and in my life. Gratitude provides you with more fuel and the strength to carry on—to sustain the journey, the healing and restoration process.

Resentment and ingratitude will literally rob you of appreciating the amazing little and precious/priceless things and moments in your life. They will rob you of living in the present and experiencing the many blessings and opportunities that it brings and holds. Therefore, do all in your ability to consciously adopt and practise gratitude daily.

A life of ingratitude and resentment will rob you of your joy and inner peace. Ingratitude does not and will never help you resolve a problem or overcome a challenge in life. It will never make you feel any better or even good, so why waste your valuable time and life in ingratitude or grief? Live and experience the present with a heart full of joy and gratitude.

CHAPTER 4

Triumphing Over Grief Through Gratitude

"A grateful heart is a cheerful one, a broken and complaining heart saps our energy."

In the previous chapters we looked at why it's so important for us to be grateful, why it's so important for us to embrace every single day as a gift- as a present. Why it's very important to acknowledge and recognise the blessings that we have in our lives and not live a life of entitlement and/or greed… thinking we deserve or are entitled to this, that, and that, and when we don't have them, we grieve, we feel pain, deep sorrow, heartache, and resentment.

Like I mentioned in the previous chapters, when we keep looking at that which we don't have, that which we have lost, the energy goes to that direction - but it's unproductive energy because we have lost what we are focussing on, and cannot retrieve it. On the other hand, when we shift our focus, attention, and energy towards the opportunities and cherished moments that our loved ones brought into our lives while they were with us—and all that continues to live within us even after they have departed from this physical world—we discover a renewed sense of life and meaning, despite their passing and the loss.

Triumphing over grief through gratitude has been explored extensively in psychological research, with numerous studies showing the benefits of gratitude for mental health, well-being, and coping with loss. Below are some key scientific findings and studies that highlight the positive impact of gratitude on overcoming grief:

1. Gratitude and Emotional Resilience:

A study conducted by Watkins et al. (2003) in the *Journal of Personality and Social Psychology* demonstrated that individuals who practised gratitude showed significantly lower levels of depression and were better able to cope with stressful events, including grief. The study found that gratitude helps individuals reframe their emotional experiences, leading to emotional resilience.

The study suggests that focusing on the positive aspects of life, even in difficult times such as grief, can help individuals move forward and find peace, promoting psychological healing.

2. Gratitude and Depression:

A study by Emmons and McCullough (2003) in *Psychological Science* showed that people who practised gratitude experienced improved psychological well-being, including reduced symptoms of depression. The study found that keeping a gratitude journal, where individuals record things they are grateful for, was particularly effective in lifting mood and reducing feelings of sadness.

For those grieving, focusing on what remains or what has been positive in their lives can help them shift focus away from their losses, leading to a reduction in depressive symptoms.

3. Gratitude and Post-Traumatic Growth:

The concept of post-traumatic growth (PTG) refers to the positive change that can occur as a result of adversity. Research has shown that gratitude plays a significant role in promoting PTG. Calhoun and Tedeschi (2006) identified gratitude as one of the key factors that help people navigate through trauma, including grief, leading to personal growth and greater appreciation for life.

The study concluded that individuals who practised gratitude were more likely to experience positive changes in their relationships, outlook on life, and sense of purpose following traumatic events, such as the loss of a loved one.

4. Gratitude and Reduced Grief Intensity:

A study published in *The Journal of Positive Psychology* in 2016 examined the role of gratitude in bereavement and found that individuals who engaged in regular gratitude exercises, such as writing down things they were thankful for, experienced a reduction in the intensity of grief. The researchers noted that while grief does not disappear, the experience of gratitude helps to transform it into a more manageable and healing process.

5. Gratitude as a Coping Mechanism:

A 2018 study by Kashdan et al. found that gratitude is an effective coping mechanism for handling loss and bereavement. The study concluded that expressing gratitude can mitigate negative emotions such as anger, resentment, and sadness during times of loss, helping individuals develop a more balanced and positive perspective.

This research supports the idea that by acknowledging and appreciating the positives in life, even in the midst of grief, individuals can begin to heal more effectively.

Conclusion:

The scientific evidence clearly shows that gratitude can be a powerful tool in triumphing over grief. Gratitude helps individuals shift their focus from what has been lost to what remains, encouraging emotional resilience, reducing depression, promoting post-traumatic growth, and enabling individuals to process their grief in healthier ways. By practising gratitude, whether through journaling or mindfulness, individuals can begin to heal emotionally, experience greater life satisfaction, and regain their sense of purpose.

These findings demonstrate that gratitude does not erase the pain of grief, but rather it provides a way to navigate through it in a manner that promotes healing, inner peace, and long-term well-being.

As we continue to unlock and explore the power of gratitude in overcoming grief, in this chapter, I would like to share with you in more detail my own personal journey and experience of overcoming grief through gratitude, highlighting the fundamental principles and supreme law that unlock the therapeutic power of gratitude as an antidote for grief. What I am about to share with you happened eight years ago, when I lost my mum– about eight years following dad's passing onto glory.

While I don't want to make this about me, I can only teach what I live and practise. My life serves as an example and testament to my authority, and I always maintain that I am not qualified to teach anything I haven't lived or practised myself.

Therefore, I will share my experiences with you, hoping it will give you the time and opportunity to reflect on your own life and see how it resonates with my journey. This is about you; it is about finding new hope whenever you feel like you've lost something valuable—your health, your job, the life you desired, your marriage, etc.

I want this to bring you renewed hope, allowing you to focus on the endless blessings and possibilities that each day brings, and to create the memories you would love to cherish forever. Let your past experiences be the building blocks that shape you into the best version of yourself yet to come.

Through my journey of overcoming grief, I have ensured that every single day I wake up, I am eternally grateful—even before I am fully awake or pray. Each morning, as I take my first breath, I start with gratitude. I am grateful for the first breath of the day, grateful for a good night's sleep, and grateful for the breath of life. This attitude has been my number one attribute to success, humility, inner peace, contentment, joy, and optimism, and I hope it inspires you to adopt this trait as well. I am aware you may already be practising this, but if you're not doing it enough, could you join me on this journey of gratitude and healing? Let's make it a lifestyle and a habit, and watch our lives transform forever.

As I mentioned in the previous chapters of this book, my mum and dad are no longer with us. I've also lost my sister and some other close relatives, but I want to specifically talk about my mum and dad. They gave me life and were used by God as vessels to bring me to this planet so I could fulfil my purpose and continue doing what I am doing now.

Dad died in Cameroon in 2006 when I was pregnant with my first daughter, so I couldn't travel back home. I was a daddy's girl. Daddy was everything to me. He meant the world to me. Daddy was my first love. He was truly amazing, kind, and showed us unconditional love. He taught me how to appreciate and value myself and others. He was one of the most incredible people I have ever known, and I believe no one can replace him. When Dad died, I thought, *oh my goodness! My life will never be the same again!* I thought my life was going to take a severe downturn. I believed I would be destroyed, damaged, and would break down.

However, on the day I received the news of Dad's passing, I was reminded about all that my dad meant to me and represented, by a very good friend of mine, my wonderful friend and colleague in Italy, Davide, a strong man of faith, who drove me home from work following the sad news. He gave me hope, reminding me of the great things I had told him about Dad. He reminded me that Dad had gone to rest from the pain of this world and from his illness, and he encouraged me to keep those memories alive. I held on to that, and guess what? I lived, and I continued to live for 15 years after Dad's death. Dad has never left me. He has never truly gone. I've never lost Dad because he continues to live in me to this very moment.

Each time you see me being super kind, loving unconditionally, or forgiving in the blink of an eye, Dad is being manifested in my life. He was one of the kindest humans I've ever known—so forgiving, loving, kind, and naive when it came to evil, yet wise, intelligent, and very humble. Whenever I'm humble, it is a reflection of Dad. I'm always humble because it's a privilege to be alive, to have all the gifts I have, and to be able to serve you.

Dad still lives in me. I overcame his death relatively quickly. In the early days following Dad's passing, I could see him in my dreams. He would show me a beautiful light that led to where he was and speak to me. I could vividly see the light and knew my dad was in a wonderful place and always with me—in my heart.

Fast forward eight years, and I was pregnant again, this time with my youngest child and last daughter. I'm not sure why I always seem to be pregnant during these difficult moments. This time was a bit different, as it was close to my due date. I lost my wonderful mum, a prayer warrior, a confidante, an unshakable woman with powerful, unwavering core convictions and faith in God. Every time you see me being fearless, powerful, courageous, and daring—that's definitely

Mum in me. I am the best blend of Mum and Dad. I always tell my siblings that I am 70% Dad and 30% Mum. 30% of Mum is capable of moving mountains. You don't need more than 30% of my mum. If you knew her, you'd understand. It's enough to move mountains. It's like having a lion leading millions of sheep; one lion is enough to transform the mindset of millions of sheep to become lions.

Mum had powerful, unshakable, unwavering faith and was a formidable prayer warrior. I don't think I'm anywhere close to her praying ability, but I believe I inherited some of her courage and daring personality. A week before my due date, Mum was buried—exactly one week before the birth of my youngest child. Mum's death, of course, brought Dad's memories back to life. However, Dad had always been living in me, and I found myself asking questions like, "Why now?"

I couldn't even say a final farewell to my mum and dad. I found myself drifting into a negative mindset, but by then, I was already deeply involved in my transformation work. I could easily and immediately shift my mindset back to where I wanted it to be—towards peace, glory, joy, and the celebration of their lives.

With Mum's passing, it was especially challenging as I was also going through some difficult times in my life—specifically in my marriage. However, God was building me up and equipping and empowering me to fulfil His purpose for my life. I give thanks for the challenges in my marriage, as they shaped me into the resilient, tenacious, compassionate, and loving woman I am today. God was working on me.

Maybe I was a little vulnerable then, but I don't want to use the word vulnerable. It was the ideal moment for God to perfect His work in my life and ensure that His true purpose for my life is fulfilled. It was just the perfect moment, and it had nothing to do with vulnerability.

As the potter works on the clay, the clay is not vulnerable when it is soft—it is in the perfect state. It has to be malleable; if it's hard, the potter would need to break it. Hence, I don't really want to say I was vulnerable. I was definitely not vulnerable. As earlier said, we are not victims. I'm not a victim. Every situation, every experience, is valuable and has the power to transform our lives and the lives of countless individuals.

I have learned to embrace experiences and seek for the lessons in them. Hence, grieving the loss of my mum was the perfect moment for God to work in me and teach me what I needed to learn. I knew that all my intelligence, knowledge, wisdom, and even strength could not help me. I had to surrender, humble myself, and look up to someone greater. God had to break me to help me understand that I needed to surrender and allow Him to work while I rested. It was the perfect moment because if I believed I could handle everything myself, I wouldn't look to God. I would think, *I can do this. My wisdom, my knowledge, my intelligence, and my strength can take care of this.* I found perfect rest in God, knowing that the outcome would be God's perfect will for my life, beautifully tailored for His unique and divine purpose.

During my moments of grief, even when I felt at my lowest, I remained fully aware that the power to rise again resided within me. In those dark days and moments, I knew I carried a light within—a light I could easily ignite. I understood where the switch was—in my mind—and all I needed to do was reach for it and turn it on when I needed it most.

I could liken these periods of despair and darkness to stepping into a dark room. You don't pray to never encounter a dark room; nor, when you find yourself in one, do you pray for the darkness to disappear or curse it. Instead, you simply locate the switch and turn on the light.

I was at a point in my life where, despite being only human and enduring a painful experience, I knew exactly where the switch was. If I needed to remain in the darkness briefly, to feel and embrace my humanity, I allowed myself that moment. I permitted my imperfect human nature to surface and be expressed. I stayed in that space without condemnation, guilt, or excuses.

However, I also knew when it was enough—when it was time to rise and turn on the light. I understood that I needed the light, not only for myself but for my children and family, for you, and for the world that relies on me. So, I would reach for the switch, turn on the light, and step forward into it once more.

Even though I grieved for Mum, there was never a moment when I completely broke down. Not once did I fail to give my all to my children and myself. Not once did I ignore the call when God summoned me to serve my children and others. Not once did I neglect to care for myself when nurturing was necessary. I understood that Mum and Dad loved me immensely and would want me to thrive and be at my best. Even though they were no longer physically present, their enduring love reminded me that I could truly overcome my grief. While I experienced moments of sorrow, I always returned swiftly to a positive, joyful, and optimistic state, filled with praise and worship.

Through pain, trials, and challenges, I remained steadfast. Remarkably, I didn't suffer a single headache throughout my pregnancy. My unborn daughter, unwavering in her strength, overcame every challenge I faced within my home and marriage. When she was born, her middle name, "Nduno," meaning "conqueror," was chosen to honour my mum. It was destiny—she truly embodied the lioness spirit of my mother, a conqueror and warrior in every sense.

On that blessed day, the 27th of August 2015, as I brought forth a new life—Destiny Nduno Likambi—I found myself thinking of the life I had lost, my mum's. In that moment, I was almost rebuked by my own thoughts: *Sylvia, come on. How ungrateful can you be?*

Here I was, lying on a hospital bed, having just given birth to a beautiful new life. I reflected: *Do you even comprehend what it takes to create a new life? Do you think it's as simple as being pregnant and giving birth? No. Is it because you deserve it or have done something extraordinary? No.*

I thought of all the women who yearn to be pregnant, even for a fleeting moment, yet are unable to conceive. And here I was, holding my third healthy child. What had I done to deserve such a blessing?

I whispered, "Nothing, Lord. Have mercy."

In that moment, I realised how truly privileged and blessed I was to serve as a vessel to bring this precious life into the world. Then, I turned my thoughts inward and questioned myself: *How dare you question the taking of a life—your mum's life—when you have just been entrusted with this incredible gift?*

A life has been taken from you, and a new life has been brought into your life. Not even just one life. You are still living; you are privileged to have your own life. Is it because you deserve it? Do you know how many women have died in childbirth? Here you are, with a healthy baby girl. You are healthy and alive, though with a few pains and hurts. Shouldn't you be grateful?

I'm having this conversation with myself, beloved. Remember, this is my work—my vocation, my profession, and my very being. Every day, I remind myself of the positive and powerful words I carry within me.

I tell myself, "Sylvia, you've got to be grateful here. You've got to be grateful.

Why focus on what you think you've lost, which, in truth, you haven't really lost? You know that Mum still lives in you. You know that Dad still lives in you. They raised you and laid the foundational pillars of your core beliefs—most of which you still uphold today. You are a representation of their values and principles. So why search for something that cannot be found, something that is no longer physically there?"

The above questions and reflection brought to mind the resurrection of Jesus. When the women went to His tomb on the third day, they were met with a profound question from the angels: *Why are you looking for someone who is alive among the dead?*

Let's delve deeper into this moment. After Jesus' crucifixion and burial, several women who had followed Him came to the tomb early on the third day to anoint His body with spices, as was customary.

However, they found the stone rolled away from the entrance and the tomb empty. As they stood bewildered, two angels, dazzling in appearance, appeared and reminded them of Jesus' prophecy: that He would rise again on the third day.

Here is the account from Luke 24:1–7:

"On the first day of the week, very early in the morning, the women took the spices they had prepared and went to the tomb. They found the stone rolled away from the tomb, but when they entered, they did not find the body of the Lord Jesus. While they were wondering about this, suddenly two men in clothes that gleamed like lightning stood beside them. In their fright, the women bowed down with their faces to the ground, but the men said to them, 'Why do you look for the living among the dead? He is not here; He has risen! Remember how He told you, while He was still with you in Galilee: "The Son of Man must be delivered over to the hands of sinners, be crucified, and on the third day be raised again."' Then they remembered His words." (Luke 24:1–7, NIV).

This shift in perspective was transformative for me. I asked myself, *Why am I still grieving? We grieve for those who are dead. Why am I grieving for someone who is still alive—alive in me and dwelling within me?* Jesus said, *"I am the resurrection and the life. The one who believes in Me will live, even though they die."* (John 11:25).

How could I be searching among the dead for Daddy William Forchap and Mama Eli Nduno Forchap, who are forever with Christ and live on in me?

Another powerful real-life example of overcoming grief through gratitude is Oprah Winfrey. Oprah has openly shared her journey of grief and how practising gratitude helped her navigate the loss of her beloved mother, Vernita Lee, who passed away in 2018. Oprah's story is a compelling testament to the transformative power of gratitude in coping with loss.

Oprah Winfrey's Journey of Grief and Gratitude:

Oprah's relationship with her mother was complex, filled with both love and tension. Despite their strained relationship at times, Oprah often spoke of the immense love she felt for her mother. When Vernita Lee passed away, Oprah was devastated, but she also recognised the importance of shifting her perspective to one of gratitude rather than solely focusing on the pain of the loss.

In her reflections, Oprah shared that she began to focus on the positive memories and lessons her mother had imparted to her throughout her life. She took time to express gratitude for the love her mother had given her, the strength she had instilled in her, and the lessons she had learned from their relationship, both the challenges and the joys. Oprah shared with her audience that the act of gratitude allowed her to feel more connected to her mother's spirit, rather than dwelling on the pain of her physical absence.

In her interviews and public statements, Oprah revealed that while the grief was still present, it was gratitude that allowed her to honour her mother's legacy and to keep her memory alive in a way that felt healing. Oprah said, "I'm grateful for the time that I had with my mother, for the lessons I learned from her, and for the way she shaped me into the person I am today." By focusing on gratitude, Oprah found a sense of peace, allowing her to grieve in a healthy way and heal emotionally.

Oprah has also shared in her books and interviews how gratitude is a core part of her daily life. Practising gratitude, for her, has been essential not just in overcoming grief but in navigating life's many challenges. By focusing on what she had gained from her relationship with her mother—rather than solely on her loss—she found a way to integrate her grief into a broader, more positive framework.

Her story highlights that even in the most difficult moments of grief, gratitude has the power to transform our perspective. Oprah's ability to focus on the positives, express gratitude for what was, and continue her healing journey despite the loss is a testament to the transformative power of gratitude in overcoming grief.

Key Takeaways:

- Gratitude helps shift focus from the pain of loss to the blessings of the relationship.
- Focusing on the positive memories and lessons learned allows for emotional healing.
- Gratitude enables us to feel connected to our loved ones, even after their passing.

Oprah's story is another powerful example of how gratitude can be a guiding light through the darkness of grief, allowing us to heal, grow, and find peace while honouring the memory of loved ones.

CHAPTER 5

The Role of Perception & Selflessness in Overcoming Grief

"If we live, we live for the Lord; and if we die, we die for the Lord. So, whether we live or die, we belong to the Lord. For this very reason, Christ died and returned to life so that he might be the Lord of both the dead and the living." Romans 14:8

"Yet what we suffer now is nothing compared to the glory he will reveal to us later." Romans 8:18

A powerful real-life example of the role of perception and selflessness in overcoming grief is seen the journey of Viktor Frankl, a psychiatrist and Holocaust survivor, whose experiences in Nazi concentration camps reshaped his understanding of suffering and grief.

Viktor Frankl was arrested by the Nazis in 1942 and sent to Auschwitz, where he endured unimaginable hardship, losing his wife, parents, and brother in the brutal conditions of the camp. In the face of extreme suffering and grief, Frankl found a profound sense of meaning and purpose in his life, which ultimately helped him survive the horrors of the Holocaust.

While in the camp, Frankl realised that although he could not control his external circumstances — the brutal treatment, the loss of his loved ones, the constant threat of death — he could control his perception of those circumstances. He made the conscious decision to choose how he responded to his suffering. Frankl observed that those prisoners who found meaning in their suffering, who focused on something beyond their pain, were more likely to survive than those who succumbed to despair.

In his book, *Man's Search for Meaning,* Frankl explains his concept of logotherapy, which emphasises the importance of finding meaning in life, even in the most challenging and painful of circumstances. Frankl wrote that "those who have a 'why' to live, can bear with almost any 'how'." For Frankl, the key to overcoming grief and suffering was not denying the pain, but choosing to find meaning and purpose in the midst of it.

One of Frankl's most profound moments of perception came when he envisioned himself giving a lecture about his experiences after the war. This vision gave him hope and the strength to continue living, even when everything around him seemed hopeless. He chose to focus on the possibility of a future, a future in which his suffering could help others find meaning in their own lives.

In the midst of his grief and loss, Frankl also experienced selflessness. His observations and insights were not solely for his own survival, but he felt a deep sense of responsibility to others who were suffering around him. He used his role as a psychiatrist to offer support and comfort to fellow prisoners, helping them cope with their suffering by encouraging them to find meaning in their lives, even in the face of such overwhelming grief.

Frankl's story teaches us how perception — choosing to focus on meaning and purpose — and selflessness — supporting others in their pain — can transform grief and suffering into something more powerful that leads to growth and healing. His ability to shift his focus from the overwhelming loss he experienced to the potential for positive action in the future allowed him to not only survive but to help others survive as well.

Viktor Frankl's journey is a profound example of how, through a shift in perception and a commitment to selflessness, one can overcome even the deepest grief. His legacy continues to inspire millions around the world to find meaning in their suffering, and to live with a renewed sense of purpose and compassion.

I heard about another story of a couple in Cameroon who experienced the devastating loss of their 10-year-old daughter, Olivia, to a rare form of cancer.

Olivia had been diagnosed with an aggressive brain tumour, and despite undergoing surgery and intensive treatment, her condition deteriorated rapidly. The couple, whose names have been withheld, faced a heart-wrenching period of uncertainty, watching their daughter fight for her life. In the midst of their unimaginable grief, the couple made a conscious decision to shift their perception of the situation and focus on something beyond their pain: honouring Olivia's memory and helping other children facing similar struggles.

Rather than falling into despair, Olivia's parents took on a selfless mission to support families who were affected by childhood cancer. With the help of donations from well-wishers and family members, they provided financial and emotional support to families in their local community who are going through similar battles. Their grief, rather than defining them, became the driving force for their actions, as they channelled their love for Olivia into helping others.

In a powerful interview, Olivia's mum explained, "In the darkest moments of our lives, we had to decide whether to let grief consume us or to honour our daughter by making something good come from her life. She would have wanted us to keep fighting, to keep helping others, and to keep her memory alive."

Their selflessness in dedicating their lives to helping other children has made a significant impact to an issue close to their hearts. Through their actions, they have exemplified how perception and selflessness can transform grief into something positive. Instead of allowing their loss to consume them, they chose to focus on their daughter's legacy and to give back to the community. Their story is one of immense strength and resilience, showing that even in the face of the most devastating loss, there is potential for hope, healing, and compassion through helping others.

Their journey has not only helped them heal but has also made a profound difference in the lives of countless other families. They turned their grief into a source of strength, demonstrating that by changing our perception of loss and choosing to act selflessly, we can rise above the pain and make a meaningful impact in the world.

In my first book, *A Father's Tender and Compassionate Love,* I wrote extensively about my father's love for me, my siblings, and everyone he encountered. Reflecting on this, alongside my encounter with the Holy Spirit and a period of deep self-reflection, I had an epiphany. I asked myself: "Sylvia, you only grieve for what you've lost. But you haven't truly lost Dad—he still lives in you. In the same way, Mum lives in you, even though she's no longer here physically. Would you rather have Dad back, alive, but in unbearable pain? Would you rather have Mum here, despite knowing she was suffering in ways you couldn't help with? And, despite being in the comfort of your home in England, you couldn't be physically there for them, nor see them? Was your desire to know they were alive, to feel comforted by the thought of them being here, truly about them?"

Although they were no longer physically with me, and knowing they were no longer in pain, the realisation that they still lived within me brought a sense of relief. Especially since I couldn't take their suffering away, I asked myself, "Shouldn't you be grateful that the Lord called them to rest, so they don't have to continue suffering in this world?"

It was a tough question, but a necessary one. I asked myself: "Would you rather be comfortable for your own selfish reasons, just wanting to know that Mum and Dad were still alive, even though you weren't there to care for them? While they were in pain, you were miles away in England. Do you want them to keep suffering in this physical world just to feed your own ego? To know they are alive, yet in so much pain? Because, in truth, this is not about Mum and Dad. Those who leave us no longer grieve. They are gone, and most of them are in a better place than they were here on earth."

If, like me, you believe in God, in Jesus, in the resurrection, then you believe your parents, your loved ones who have passed on, are in a better place. There is a greater hope. I felt the Holy Spirit speaking to me: "You know the tribulations you go through daily—the pain of your physical body, your health, mental and physical. You are aware that they are finally resting in peace, resting in the Lord—not dead. Why, then, are you continuing to grieve? Why are you resentful? Why are you not thankful for the new life I've given you? Why aren't you focusing on caring for the life I've entrusted to you—your own life? Your own mental and physical well-being? Why grieve for someone I have in my care, resting in my presence?"

As I reflected on these words, and on my actions and perceptions surrounding my mum's passing—which also brought back memories of Dad's—I realised how ungrateful I had been. I had been focused on what I had lost, forgetting to see the endless blessings I had been given.

I thought of the three beautiful children I had been privileged to bring into the world. I thought of my own life, my own health. Immediately, a shift occurred in my mindset—a change of perception—from loss to gain, from death to life. I began to celebrate life—my life, my newborn baby, my children, my family, and my husband.

Every breath I took became a moment of gratitude. The fact that I was lying healthy on that hospital bed after delivering my third healthy child, still alive to care for my children—I was immensely grateful for. I shifted my mindset in that moment. The grieving was over. It was done. There was a new awakening, a new revolution, a new life—Mum living in me.

I began to count my blessings, to praise God. And right there in that hospital bed, I began to sing. I smiled as I sang:

"Count your blessings, name them one by one,
Count your blessings, see what God has done,
Count your blessings, name them one by one,
And it will surprise you what the Lord has done..."

In that moment, my grief was replaced with deep, abiding gratitude. I had shifted my perception from loss to abundance, from death to life. The love of my parents, though no longer physical, still lived in me—and for that, I was eternally thankful.

I hope my journey inspires you to change your perception about death and turn to gratitude in the midst of your grief and pain.

At this point, I would like to pause and say this to you, beloved: as you continue reading, I encourage you to take a moment, grab a blank sheet of paper, and begin to count your blessings. Name them one by one, write them down, and number them. Keep counting your blessings and acknowledging what God has done in your life. Count your blessings, beloved, name them one by one, and it will surprise you what the Lord has done.

I think it's fitting for me to end with this song. I will remain still; I will say no more. I won't sing it for you (as that's not possible in a book, anyway). Instead, I'll share the words here so you can read them, open your heart, and let them sink deeply into your soul, especially when you're thinking of your loss. It could be the loss of your health, your loved one, or your relationship with your child—the relationship you've always dreamed of but don't have. Maybe you've lost that incredible connection with your child or even with yourself.

I want you to take a moment to count your blessings and be grateful for what you have in your life. These blessings will multiply, and you'll attract even more blessings and people who share the same positive energy—they will come into your heart.

By embracing gratitude, you will open the door to many more blessings, possibilities, and hope. Don't dwell on the past, or on the pain of yesterday. Don't dwell on the loss of a loved one. They are alive in you now. Please allow me to share this with you: I completely respect and value you. You may not share my beliefs, and that's okay—take from this song and message whatever resonates with you.

Now, let's go:

When upon life's billows you are tempest-tossed,
When you are discouraged, thinking all is lost,

Count your many blessings, name them one by one,
And it will surprise you what the Lord has done.

Count your blessings, name them one by one,
Count your blessings, see what God has done!
Count your blessings, name them one by one,
And it will surprise you what the Lord has done.

Are you ever burdened with a load of care?
Does the cross seem heavy you are called to bear?
Count your many blessings, every doubt will fly,
And you will be singing as the days go by.

Count your blessings, name them one by one,
Count your blessings, see what God has done!
Count your blessings, name them one by one,
And it will surprise you what the Lord has done.

When you look at others with their lands and gold,
Think that Christ has promised you His wealth untold;
Count your many blessings, money cannot buy
Your reward in heaven, nor your home on high.

Count your blessings, name them one by one,
Count your blessings, see what God has done!
Count your blessings, name them one by one,
And it will surprise you what the Lord has done.

So, amid the conflict, whether great or small,
Do not be discouraged, God is over all;
Count your many blessings, angels will attend,
Help and comfort give you to your journey's end.

Count your blessings, name them one by one,
Count your blessings, see what God has done!
Count your blessings, name them one by one,
And it will surprise you what the Lord has done.

Now, let's continue in gratitude. Today, I invite you to walk with me through this journey of thankfulness. Open your heart and let go of the past, embracing this present moment as the precious gift it truly is.

We have countless reasons to be grateful for: the gift of life, health, and well-being bestowed upon us by the grace of God. Let us shift our focus from what we lack to the abundance of blessings that surround us. Join me in a spirit of gratitude as we count our blessings, appreciating the priceless gifts that money could never buy. In the preceding chapters, I shared how gratitude transformed my life, guiding me away from grief and towards true appreciation for all that I've been given.

Now, let's elevate our gratitude to a new dimension. Let's recognise the richness that even past losses have brought into our lives. As we embrace gratitude, let us welcome the abundance and blessings that await us.

CHAPTER 6

Decoding The Supreme Law of Gratitude

Unlocking the gateway to Divine Healing and Restoration

"To unlock the gateway to Divine Healing and Restoration, we must surrender our brokenness, trust in the infinite grace of the Creator, and allow His unconditional love to restore what was lost, renew what was broken, and heal what was wounded."

As we further explore the Supreme Law of Gratitude, I want us to see another dimension of gratitude and it's infinite potential to heal us. In this chapter, we will delve into the divine law and healing power of gratitude, recognising it as the foundation of a life filled with meaning, purpose, and abundance.

As we have seen throughout this book, gratitude is far more than a mere polite gesture or momentary emotion; it is a deep recognition and acknowledgment of the abundant blessings that enrich our lives. Gratitude serves as a supreme law and a key, unlocking the gateway to infinite opportunities as well as divine healing and restoration. It invites us to welcome into our lives all that we wish to have, become, and experience.

Now, let us take a moment to spell out the word "GRATITUDE" as we uncover the infinite healing potential and hidden treasures contained within it. Write the word "GRATITUDE" clearly before you.

G in gratitude represents **GIFT** and **GRACE**.

R in gratitude represents **RECOGNITION**

A in gratitude represents **ABUNDANCE**

T in gratitude represents **TRUST**

I in gratitude represents **INTENTION**

T in gratitude represents **THANKSGIVING**

U in gratitude represents **UNITY**

D in gratitude represents **DESTINY**

E in gratitude represents **ENLIGHTENMENT**

1. The Law of the Gift and Grace of Life

"Every breath we take is a gift of grace. Every heartbeat, undeserved".
John Piper

"For it is by grace you have been saved, through faith—and this is not from yourselves, it is the gift of God— not by works, so that no one can boast." Ephesians 2:8-9

I would like to start off this section by offering a simple definition of gift and grace, respectively.

A gift is defined as a thoughtful expression of care, given voluntarily without expecting anything in return.

On the other hand, Grace is defined as the unmerited and undeserved kindness and favour shown to someone, often coming from a place of compassion, forgiveness, or generosity.

The grace of God refers to the unearned, unconditional, and undeserved favour, kindness, and mercy that God shows to humanity. It signifies God's love, forgiveness, and compassion towards us despite our imperfections and shortcomings.

At the heart of gratitude lies the recognition that the life that we have today is a gift—a precious and priceless gift bestowed upon us by the divine grace of the Almighty. Each breath we take, each beat of our hearts, is a reflection to the profound generosity of the Almighty God. It is by grace that we were chosen to receive this precious gift of life, with all its infinite healing potentials and possibilities.

As you read these words, I encourage you to take a moment and imagine the complex circumstances and events that had to align perfectly for you and me to exist in this moment—yet to be deciphered by science. From the dawn of time to the present day, countless generations have come and gone, each playing their part in building humanity—some living life fully and accomplishing purpose, with others robbing themselves of life and being unfulfilled—dying empty and void. And yet, here you are, here I am, a living, breathing testament to the miracle and grace of life and existence. What greater gift could there be than the gift of life itself?

What then is the purpose of the gift of life? Why are we offered this priceless gift without our consent? It seems as though this it forced on us, with or without our approval or prior knowledge. The gift of life is bestowed upon us with a purpose—a divine purpose that calls us to fulfil our highest potential and contribute our unique gifts to the world. Just as a manufacturer or inventor manufactures or creates each product or creation with a specific purpose in mind, so too are we created and born with a definite purpose in God's mind that is uniquely ours to fulfil.

It is not enough to merely exist; we are called to live fully and purposefully—to embrace each moment with gratitude and to seize every opportunity with courage and conviction. Hence, to truly appreciate the gift of life, we must first understand its purpose—for nothing is created, given life, or manufactured without purpose, and so too are we created and gifted life with a purpose in mind.

Therefore, it is paramount that we nurture and care for this unique gift of life in order to maximise its potential. Just as we would care for a precious gift entrusted to our care, so too must we care for the gift of life bestowed upon us. Our health, our well-being—all the incredible gifts we have been privileged to receive—are ours to cherish, nurture, care for, and protect. Simply put, our bodies and souls require care and attention to function at their best.

Let's consider the analogy of a brand-new car. When we are given a new car, we take care to maintain it—to service it regularly, to keep it clean and well-maintained. Nonetheless, when it comes to our own bodies and minds, we often end up neglecting the care and attention they require. We sometimes push ourselves to the brink of exhaustion, we indulge in unhealthy habits, including continuous and unhealthy grief, and we ignore the warning signs that our bodies and minds are sending us.

However, when we truly appreciate the gifts we have been given—when we acknowledge their value and importance—we are inspired to care for them with love and diligence. We nourish our bodies with healthy food and exercise, we nurture our minds with positive and healthy thoughts and affirmations, and we honour the divine spark and spirit within us that yearns to shine brightly in the world.

Counting Our Gifts and Blessings

In the turmoil of daily life, it is easy to lose sight of the countless gifts and blessings that surround us. We become so focused on what we do not have that we forget to appreciate what we do have—the endless gifts and blessings that enrich our lives in both big and small ways.

By pausing to count our gifts and blessings, and expressing gratitude in the moment, we grant ourselves permission to shift our perspective—to turn our attention away from lack, scarcity, and death towards abundance and life. I challenge you to pause: count your blessings, name them one by one, and write them down. Experience the richness of life in all its countless forms. When we are truly grateful for what we have, we open ourselves to receive even more blessings in return.

So, I invite you now to join me in counting our gifts—to acknowledge the countless blessings that enrich our lives each day. From the gift of life itself to the treasures of friendship, family, and love, let us celebrate the abundance that surrounds us and embrace each moment with gratitude and joy.

Finally, I want to take this opportunity to remind you that expressing gratitude for the gift and grace of life is a treasure beyond measure—a precious and unquenchable light that shines brightly, even in the darkest times. It reminds us of the boundless abundance around us and invites us to embrace each moment with open arms and an open heart.

Let us cultivate a spirit of gratitude in our lives and never forget the infinite gifts and blessings that enrich us daily. For truly, the gift of life is the greatest gift of all.

2. The Law of Recognition

Recognition can be defined as acknowledging or showing appreciation for our gifts, qualities, achievements, or contributions and that of others. Recognition and acknowledgment birth gratitude and vice versa.

Recognition goes beyond acknowledging a single act of kindness—a transitory moment of acknowledgment. It is a constant and deliberate act—an intentional shift in perspective and lifestyle that allows us to see the world differently—through eyes of gratitude and love. When we take the time to recognise the gifts that we have been given—to truly appreciate their value and importance—despite the challenges and hardships we encounter, we open ourselves up to healing and a deeper sense of serenity. The later empowers us to express more gratitude and appreciation for the richness of life.

In life, recognition plays a vital role—a role that extends beyond simple acknowledgment. It represents the foundation upon which gratitude is built, the catalyst that propels us towards a deeper understanding of the gift of life and the endless blessings that enrich our lives. In the following paragraphs, we delve deeper into the transformational power of recognition and acknowledgement, embracing them as indispensable pillars in our journey towards healing and a life of purpose, meaning, and abundance.

When we don't recognise and acknowledge our gifts, we become ungrateful. When we are ungrateful, we fail to recognise and acknowledge the enormous blessings and gifts we have been given. Our focus shifts to what we lack, to what is dead, to what we think we are entitled to but do not have. On the other hand, when we recognise our gifts, acknowledge our blessings and the grace upon our lives, we become more grateful and fulfilled.

At the heart of gratitude lies the recognition of the countless gifts and blessings that grace our lives each and every day. Notwithstanding, in our pursuit of happiness and fulfilment, it is all too easy to overlook these blessings—to become so focused on what we do not have that we fail to recognise the abundance that surrounds us.

Below are examples of some of the endless gifts we have been blessed with, that I invite you to pause, recognise, and acknowledge daily.

i. The Gift of Presence

In our fast-paced world, time is a precious commodity—a gift that is often taken for granted. Yet, when we pause to acknowledge our presence and the presence of others—to recognise the gift of our time and their time and attention—we honour ourselves, others, and the sacred bond that connects us all. Whether it is a friend, family member, loved one, or a stranger passing by, each person we encounter brings with them a unique gift: the gift of their presence, just as we bring the gift of ours.

This gift of presence—whether theirs or ours—should never be taken for granted while they are with us or we are with them. These moments often live within us or them long after we or they are gone.

Let us take a moment to recognise and appreciate our presence and the presence of those around us—to acknowledge the gift of time and attention shared. Take a sheet of paper or your gratitude notebook and write down the gifts you bring through your presence and how these enrich the lives of those around you. Then, write the names of all those who have blessed or continue to bless you with the gift of their presence and how this has enriched your life.

In doing so, we value and honour the inherent worth and dignity of our lives and the lives of others, cultivating a spirit of gratitude that enriches us all. It is hard or almost impossible to bless others with our presence while we grief in unhealthy ways—because the truth is, we are not fully present—our minds, thoughts and physical being are with what or whom we have lost—we have drifted away from the present moment and are dwelling in some place or world, with the one/s we have lost. Hence, let's be present—let's embrace the present moment and live fully in the moment, recognising and appreciating the presence of those around us while also blessing them with our presence.

ii. The Gift of Knowledge

In our quest for knowledge and understanding—especially of our pain and grief—we often overlook the gift of discernment that lies within ourselves and those around us. This untapped potential, waiting to be unleashed, is a treasure of wisdom capable of transforming our lives in profound ways, particularly when we struggle to make sense of our suffering or loss.

As you read these words, I invite you to pause for a moment, close your eyes, and reflect on the immense power of the human mind.

Consider its infinite capacity for learning, growth, creativity, and innovation—qualities embedded in the complex depths of our DNA and the vast expanse of our consciousness. These gifts uniquely connect us to divine wisdom, especially during moments of uncertainty, loss, or grief, when clarity seems beyond reach.

During times of profound despair, recognising and tapping into this divine knowledge and wisdom empowers us, granting clarity, strength, and the courage to move forward. In such moments, it is vital to seek the word and knowledge of God, which provide an anchor when we feel lost and unable to connect the dots between our past, present, and future.

By seeking divine wisdom, we gain the ability to better understand and navigate our loss and grief. Surrounding ourselves with wise and knowledgeable individuals or professionals is equally important. These are people who not only offer comfort and solace but also impart profound insights that enlighten us, enabling us to see beyond our current pain and despair.

Let us, therefore, not only recognise and appreciate the gift of knowledge but also actively explore it in all its dimensions, embracing the limitless possibilities and life lessons to be uncovered. By honouring the divine wisdom within ourselves and those around us, we unlock the full potential of our being and open ourselves to a deeper understanding of the infinite opportunities for growth that lie beyond our pain, grief, and stagnation.

iii. The Gift of Potential

At the very core of your soul and DNA lies a seed—a tiny, often unnoticeable seed that holds the incredible potential for greatness. This seed is a gift, entrusted to you by the divine hand of creation, carrying the promise of abundance and prosperity.

Like all gifts, this seed of potential must be recognised, acknowledged, and nurtured to grow and flourish. When we fail to see the gifts within us—when we overlook the boundless potential residing in the seed of our being—we deny ourselves the chance to fully embrace our purpose and destiny.

Let us take a moment to recognise and appreciate this gift of potential. Honour the unique talents and abilities that make you who you are, and embrace the journey of self-discovery and growth. By doing so, you open the door to a future filled with possibilities—a future where your greatest dreams and aspirations can become reality, even beyond your current challenges and despair.

I pause here to reflect on the gifts I have been blessed with: the gift of knowledge and wisdom from God, which enables me to serve you through the words in this book and my various teachings and work.

These are gifts I do not take for granted. They are not solely the result of extensive study but are part of the divine design, embedded within me from conception. We have all been equipped with everything we need to become who we were created to be, yet many of us only recognise and use a small fraction of our full potential, operating far below our capacity.

When you begin to recognise your gifts, you see how truly rich you are. To recognise and acknowledge this richness is to understand that being rich means possessing an abundance of something valuable. How could we ever be ungrateful when we have been blessed with so many gifts? When you realise how much potential you have, you understand that you already have everything you need to fulfil your purpose in life. You don't need to look far, because all that you need to become all you were created to be, to live a purposeful and fulfilling life, is already within you. It is encoded in your unique DNA, making you one of a kind. Yet, we often fail to pause and appreciate what we have and the untapped potential within. We are too busy chasing what we lack or comparing ourselves to others, forgetting to value our own gifts and the grace upon our lives.

I see you; I recognise your infinite potential. I appreciate you, and I value you. Recognise your worth and value yourself too, for within you lies the seed of extraordinary potential. Allow me to offer a simple example. If you have heard me speak or listened to my teachings, you'll know that I often use metaphors and analogies. Imagine I place an orange seed in your hand. I am giving you a gift—an orange seed. You didn't ask for it; I simply walk up to you and place it in your hand. Now, you have an orange seed.

What have I given you? I have given you the seed of an orange fruit, but for it to produce an endless supply of oranges, you need to sow and nurture it.

Even though you hold only a seed right now, you don't need to look far to bring forth oranges—the oranges are within the seed. If you plant it in fertile soil and nurture it daily, it will sprout in due season, grow into an orange tree, and eventually bear fruits. In time, during the harvest season, that single tree will yield oranges year after year. From the fruits of that single seed, you'll gain more seeds, allowing you to plant even more orange trees, which in turn will produce countless oranges.

However, if you leave the seed on a shelf in your living room or hold it in your hand indefinitely, its potential remains untapped. By failing to recognise the power within the seed, you miss out on the greatness it could bring. You might see others with abundant oranges and feel ungrateful, thinking, *I only have an orange seed.*

We often fail to recognise the vast potential within the gifts we already have. That single orange seed has the capacity to produce trees whose fruits offer enormous health benefits—not just for you, but for many others as well. By nurturing the seed, you could create abundance to share. Yet, if you disregard the potential of that seed and let ingratitude take hold, you might even throw it away, thinking, *What can I do with just a single seed?* This is how some of us waste our lives—by failing to be grateful and to recognise the gifts and untapped potential we have been blessed with.

So today, I invite you to join me in recognising the endless potential you have been given. Embrace them, nurture them, and watch as they grow into something extraordinary. Embracing this understanding shifts your perspective from scarcity to abundance. It helps you to see that you are equipped with unique talents and capabilities that can be harnessed to achieve your goals and dreams. This realisation brings a profound sense of gratitude and contentment, allowing you to focus on nurturing and utilising your inherent gifts. As you cultivate this mindset, you will find that your life becomes more enriched and purposeful, grounded in the recognition of your inner wealth and the limitless possibilities it presents.

In conclusion, the ability to recognise and acknowledge is an immensely powerful tool—one that can transform our lives in profound and meaningful ways. When we take the time to recognise the gifts we have been given—to appreciate our own presence and the presence of others, to value the wisdom within us, and to embrace the potential at our fingertips—we open ourselves to a world of endless possibilities and opportunities.

Let us, therefore, embrace the power of recognition and acknowledgement. Cultivate a spirit of gratitude that enriches your life and the lives of those around you. In doing so, we honour the inherent worth and dignity of each individual and unlock the door to a future filled with purpose, meaning, and abundance.

3. The Law of Abundance

"Acknowledging the good that you already have in your life is the foundation for all abundance." Eckhart Tolle

"Be thankful for what you have; you'll end up having more. If you concentrate on what you don't have, you will never, ever have enough" Oprah Winfrey

By recognising and embracing our gifts and potential, we open ourselves to a mindset of abundance, enabling us to live a life filled with gratitude, trust, and endless possibilities.

Abundance is defined as having a plentiful and overflowing amount of something, whether it be material wealth, resources, opportunities, love, joy, or any other positive aspect of life. It represents a state of prosperity, richness, and fullness in various areas of our existence.

When we recognise the richness within us, rather than focus on the loss and emptiness life may bring, we begin to experience abundance. Our mindset shifts, and we adopt a renewed perspective of abundance. We begin to see ourselves in the following ways:

- I am more than enough because I embody abundance.
- I have everything I need to fulfil my purpose and live the life I was placed on earth to live.
- My gifts and riches are overflowing, and I can freely and continuously give without limits.

Personally, I don't need to hold on tightly to my gifts or always demand compensation for them. I serve freely because I have freely received. Understanding that I am rich and live in abundance reassures me that I will never run short or lack. By giving from the abundance and overflow of my gifts, I receive even more. Indeed, it is more blessed to give than to receive.

Conversely, when we are ungrateful and fail to recognise and acknowledge our gifts, we cannot comprehend how rich and wealthy we are or realise that we embody abundance. We are unaware of the fact that we already have more than enough to fulfil our purpose in life.

As a result, we hold onto things out of fear—afraid to let go or to give, because we think we will run out. We become reluctant to share and cling to what we have.

Imagine I give you the orange seed I mentioned earlier. If you close your hand tightly around it, afraid to plant it in the soil, you'll lose sight of the seed's true potential. You might think planting it means losing the only seed you have. Yet, by failing to plant it, you miss the opportunity to see how the soil nurtures and nourishes the seed, bringing forth an abundance of oranges and countless new seeds.

Sometimes, we hold onto our loved ones, last meal or our final resources, fearing we'll have nothing left. I invite you to join me in opening your hands to receive freely. We need to let go to make room for abundance in our lives.

Some of us even hesitate to receive, limited by the belief that receiving comes with strings attached. We suspect that when someone offers us a gift, they expect something in return. But we often fail to realise that those who give freely do so because they have more than enough.

When I give from my abundance and overflow and you refuse to receive, it makes no difference to me. My abundance continues to overflow. Whether or not you accept, my giving remains fruitful—it falls to the ground, grows, and produces more in its season of harvest.

Sometimes, people refuse to receive because they struggle to believe in the concept of giving freely. They think it is too good to be true because they themselves feel unable to give freely. However, God gives to us freely, and when we freely receive, we are then able to freely give to others.

When we understand that we live a life of abundance through our connection to source, we can better appreciate the importance of letting go and pouring out to keep our vessels ready to receive more. Once you are connected to the source—God, the giver of life and grace—you receive constantly. God is the source of abundance, hence, being connected to him means we can never run out or lack.

When you recognise your gifts and your richness, you understand that you already have more than enough. You realise that you possess an abundance of everything you need. This mindset fosters trust in every situation, every circumstance, and every stage of your journey.

> *"Your gratitude is magnetic, and the more gratitude you have, the more abundance you magnetize. It is Universal law!"*
> *Rhonda Byrne*

4. The Law of Trust

"My flesh and my heart may fail, but God is the strength of my heart and my portion forever." Psalm 73:26

"There is a time for everything, and a season for every activity under the heavens: a time to be born and a time to die, a time to plant and a time to uproot, a time to kill and a time to heal, a time to tear down and a time to build, a time to weep and a time to laugh, a time to mourn and a time to dance," Ecclesiastes 3:1-4

Trust is a firm belief in the reliability, truth, ability, or strength of someone or something. It involves confidence, faith, and a willingness to rely on or confide in God, our inner strength and wisdom, or another person based on a sense of security and dependability.

Trust is a fundamental pillar in navigating times of uncertainty, despair, and grief, providing a sense of security, connection, and support. In uncertain times, trust in oneself, God, and others can offer reassurance and stability, guiding us through unknown circumstances with confidence and resilience. Trust enables us to lean on reliable sources for guidance, encouragement, and direction, helping us to face challenges with assurance and hope.

The loss of loved ones takes us on an unfamiliar and unexpected journey, one where we are called to trust God more deeply than we ever have before. It is an opportunity to place our faith in His masterplan for our lives, embracing the path and process that lead us to fulfil it. Imagine yourself as clay in the hands of a skilled potter. Would you not trust the potter and the process he uses to reveal your splendour and magnificence? When the potter moulds and shapes the clay, pulling and stretching it into different forms and shapes, we must believe that he knows best. The potter works with a master design in mind, carefully crafting the clay into the special vessel it is destined to become.

To become the unique vessel He has preordained, you must undergo the process of moulding. At times, the potter may need to pull and stretch you, and though it may feel painful or overwhelming, the experience is imbued with meaning and purpose. You may be pressed, shaken, and reshaped, but this is all part of the divine process.

Trust the potter. Trust God. He is preparing and refining you, shaping you with care and intention, so that you may fulfil the extraordinary purpose He has set before you.

During moments of despair and grief, trust plays a vital role in providing comfort, understanding, and a sense of belonging. Trust in God, loved ones, friends, or support systems allows us to share our feelings, seek help, and receive compassion and empathy during difficult times. This bond of trust fosters unity and support, helping us to feel less isolated and more connected, even amidst despair. It's an opportunity to reflect on relationships that have shaped us— parents, siblings, friends—who came into our lives as unforeseen blessings. By acknowledging and expressing gratitude for the richness they brought and the lessons they imparted, we preserve the treasures they shared, allowing them to guide us through our darkest moments.

As we cultivate an attitude of gratitude, we also learn to trust the journey, God, and our ability to triumph over life's storms. We deepen our understanding that every twist and turn, every challenge faced, serves a purpose in shaping us and our unique path. We learn to acknowledge and appreciate this profound truth about life. We trust the process, even when faced with loss—whether it is friends departing, jobs slipping away, or the passing of loved ones, like my own beloved parents. These experiences, though painful, mould us into stronger, more resilient, and confident men and women of purpose. They empower and transform us to inspire and guide others on their journeys through loss and grief.

In moments of despair, when life seems to go off course, trust in the process and divine purpose becomes our anchor. It helps us to see the good around us and ahead of us, even in tough times. When we are thankful, we trust that things will get better, no matter how difficult they seem. Like a seed transforming into fruit, we trust in the unfolding of our destiny. This trust opens our eyes to the wealth and boundless potential within us, inspiring us to express gratitude for every facet of our journey.

"When one door of happiness closes, another opens; but often we look so long at the closed door that we do not see the one which has been opened for us." – Helen Keller.

I often share with others how I overcame the loss of my mum and dad through the simple yet powerful act of gratitude. I realised that while I was grieving and mourning what I had lost, my focus was entirely on their death and departure. In doing so, I failed to see their legacy—the values, lessons, and love—that continues to live and flourish in me and in everything I do.

As I mentioned earlier in this book, when my mum passed away, I was on the point of giving birth to my youngest child. Just a week after her funeral, I welcomed a beautiful, healthy baby girl into the world. Yet, despite this miraculous new life, I found myself yearning for my mum's presence and bearing the weight of her absence. As humans, we are naturally inclined to dwell on our losses rather than celebrate our blessings. However, I invite you to join me in recognising and trusting the ever-changing seasons of life, embracing the transformations they bring, and finding purpose even in the darkest of times.

We must learn to appreciate that darkness, too, serves a purpose. We cannot have daylight 24 hours a day. Just as daylight has its role, so does night. For instance, we typically wouldn't sleep with the lights on in our bedrooms because we need the darkness for rest, rejuvenation, and growth. Similarly, seeds must be sown into the ground—hidden from sunlight—to receive nourishment and grow.

Whenever I step into a dark room, I don't curse the darkness or wish it away. Instead, I simply reach for the switch and turn on the light. Because I know where the switch is and understand its purpose, I can illuminate a dark room without feeling burdened or distressed. And when I need the darkness, I simply turn off the light. The same switch has the power to bring either light or darkness, depending on what is needed at that moment.

When I was grieving my mum, I realised I had a choice to make. I could focus on my loss, or I could celebrate her life. I could dwell on death, or I could embrace life. I could allow grief to consume me, or I could let life revive and restore my strength. The "switch" to move from one perspective or experience to another was in my mind—it was about my mindset. All I needed to do was switch from death to life, from loss to gain, from grief and ingratitude to gratitude, from darkness to light, and from despair to hope.

Loss is the opposite of gain, just as grief contrasts with joy, and ingratitude with gratitude. When we grieve, we focus on what we have lost rather than what we have gained. Consequently, prolonged grieving births, nurtures, and sustains ingratitude, sorrow, and resentment. While I do not wish to label anyone as "ungrateful," as this is not the goal or purpose of this book, I must share the truth—irrespective of how you and I feel or think about it.

Lying in that hospital bed with my newborn daughter, I questioned my feelings. I thought to myself, *Sylvia, how ungrateful can you be? You have been blessed with new life—a new baby. Your mum fulfilled her purpose and is now resting in peace. She lives on in you and your daughter. Don't forget to recognise the gift of your child and express gratitude for her life. Be thankful your mum gave birth to you and that you can expand her legacy.*

Reflecting on these thoughts, I realised how privileged and blessed I was. I began to focus on my blessings, counting them one by one. This shift in mindset transformed my grief into gratitude. I recognised the gifts my mum had given me—life, unconditional love, and care, and so much more. She served her purpose, and because of her, I am alive, and my daughter has the chance to be born and live.

For those grieving or struggling with mental health challenges, don't allow yourself to be consumed by grief, as this may cause depression and worsen your mental health and wellbeing. The word *depression* implies being pressed down, drained of energy. Gratitude, however, revives and reignites your spirit. Step into gratitude and envision the abundant mental state you desire. You have been given a spirit of sound mind, love, power, and courage—not a depressed mind.

Trust the process. Every situation and challenge is working for your good. Like the orange seed I mentioned earlier, you may still see yourself as that seed, unaware of your full potential. But as you begin to recognise your gifts, you start to realise your greatness. With a little refinement, you can become outstanding, allowing your transformation to experience its full course so that you can become everything you were created to become.

Trust the process, even when friends leave, jobs are lost, or loved ones pass away. Understand that these experiences shape you into a more resilient, grateful person, capable of inspiring others on their journeys.

5. The Law of Intention

"Nobody finishes well by accident. An unintentional life accepts everything and does nothing. An intentional life embraces only the things that will add to the mission of significance" John C. Maxwell

Intention is the purpose, aim, or objective behind our thoughts, decisions, or actions. Being intentional refers to the deliberate, conscious effort to act with clarity and focus towards achieving a specific goal or desired outcome. It involves mindfulness, planning, and commitment to ensure that our actions are aligned with our values, priorities, and aspirations. Being intentional often involves taking proactive steps, making thoughtful choices, and staying true to our intentions in order to create meaningful and purposeful impact in various aspects of life.

Gratitude is not something that happens by chance. It requires intentionality. You cannot simply read this book, put it down, and then carry on with your day as usual. You must consciously decide where to direct your focus and energy. Be deliberate in what you want to experience and cultivate in your life.

Make a deliberate effort to focus on gratitude and the abundance it brings to your life. Say to yourself, "I want more of this. I want to experience more of this. I want to be thankful in every situation." Even when a spouse walks away, be thankful for the gifts they brought into your life. Appreciate the growth and maturity their presence and eventual departure provided. Embrace the opportunity to spend time alone, to understand yourself better, and to recognise that being alone is not the same as being lonely.

I invite you to join me in being intentional. Every morning, wake up and write down at least five things you are grateful for. If you can find more than ten, even better, but do not settle for less than five. Be intentional about expressing gratitude every moment of your life. Even when it feels like everything is lost, be grateful for having had the gift in the first place.

"Attention energizes, and intention transforms". Deepak Chopra

By intentionally and deliberately expressing gratitude, we can overcome the pain and sorrow of grief by shifting our focus towards the positive aspects of our lives. When we actively practice gratitude, especially in times of grief, we train our minds to recognise, acknowledge and appreciate the blessings we still have amidst the loss. This intentional act helps us cultivate a sense of appreciation for the moments of joy, love, and support that we receive from others.

Expressing gratitude intentionally also allows us to build resilience and emotional strength by finding moments of light and hope in the darkness of grief. By focusing on what we are grateful for, we can gradually shift our perspective from feelings of despair to feelings of appreciation and comfort. This deliberate practice can help us reframe our thoughts, foster a sense of connection with others, and find solace in the midst of pain.

Furthermore, this intentional act of gratitude can also help us find meaning and purpose in our experiences of loss, allowing us to honour the memories of those we have lost while embracing the love and support that surrounds us.

Consequently, by intentionally and deliberately expressing gratitude, we can overcome the pain and sorrow of grief by fostering a sense of appreciation, resilience, and emotional connection that helps us navigate the grieving process with grace, find moments of light in the darkness, and uplifts our spirits and strengthens our ability to heal.

I invite you to step into your intentions, envisioning your future and your desired life beyond grief and despair. Intentions are driven by your vision and ideal life. Yes, you may have lost a job, but what is the ideal situation you want right now? What is the ideal job? The ideal is always something better than your past or current reality; it is always a place where there is peace, harmony, and fulfilment. Your ideal could never be less than your present state. When you are intentional about your ideal, about your richness, your abundance, and your gifts, you set yourself on a path of positive transformation.

6. The Law of Thanksgiving

"Oh give thanks to the LORD, for He is good; for His steadfast love endures forever". Hebrews 12:28.

"The heart that gives thanks is a happy one, for we cannot feel thankful and unhappy at the same time". Douglas Wood

Join me in embracing an attitude of thanksgiving. Let us begin each morning with gratitude in our hearts, giving thanks and singing praises. Even when life feels challenging, let us continue in gratitude, for it elevates us to a higher spiritual realm, renewing our connection to the divine, and bringing joy into our hearts.

Thanksgiving brings unity, redefines our perspective, and aligns us in harmony—body, spirit, and soul. In this state of wholeness, we become complete, fully embracing our spiritual essence. Together, let us draw closer to our divine nature and Creator, uniting with Him. In this unity, God reveals our destiny, helping us see ourselves as He sees us—beautiful, courageous, valued, successful, cherished, and resilient, no matter our current struggles or despair.

When we lack gratitude or dwell in grief, a part of us becomes lost in what we have lost. We disconnect from our true selves and from God. Thanksgiving, however, reopens the door to the spiritual realm, allowing us to reconnect with the depths of our soul. It fosters harmony within ourselves, restoring our unity with the Creator. When we are aligned in this way, there is no inner discord. In this state of unity, God whispers truths about our being and unveils our divine purpose. He reveals our destiny, inviting us to embrace our highest potential.

Thanksgiving not only connects us to our inner self but also lifts us to a higher spiritual plane. This elevation allows us to rise above our immediate circumstances and grasp the greater purpose behind life's challenges. Walking in thanksgiving enables us to tap into an infinite well of spiritual abundance. Our God is a God of abundance—He embodies completeness, divinity, and omnipresence. Through thanksgiving, we align with this abundance, fulfilling our true purpose and living in harmony with Him. We come to see that every experience—whether joyful or painful—is part of His divine plan shaping us into our best selves.

The Power of a Thankful Heart

Just as a child expressing love and gratitude evokes a parent's desire to give more, a heart full of thanksgiving attracts blessings. Thanksgiving creates a positive energy that resonates with God's divine plan, drawing goodness into our lives. It transforms our perspective, becoming the lens through which we view the world. It fills us with peace, contentment, and a renewed sense of purpose.

Additionally, the practice of thanksgiving significantly impacts our mental and emotional well-being. Studies show that people who regularly express gratitude—through singing, speaking, or reflecting—experience greater joy and resilience. They are less prone to depression and enjoy a brighter, more fulfilling outlook on life. In a study in 2018 by Wong et al. on individuals receiving mental health support, it was found that those who wrote gratitude letters alongside therapy sessions demonstrated marked improvements in emotional recovery while those who wrote about negative experiences reported higher levels of depression and anxiety.

By nurturing positive emotions and rebalancing brain chemistry, gratitude offers a transformative path toward emotional healing and resilience. It reduces mental distress while boosting physical vitality, demonstrating the deep connection between our emotional and physical health.

Make Thanksgiving a Daily Habit

Incorporate songs of thanksgiving into your routine. Singing and verbalising gratitude not only uplift the spirit but also strengthen your connection to God. These practices illuminate the mind, bring joy to the heart, and infuse life with positivity.

Embrace thanksgiving as a way of life, a compass guiding you through difficulties. It lifts you to a spiritual realm where you are united with your true self and the divine. In this state of unity, you uncover your destiny and live a life of purpose, abundance, and peace.

Thank you for joining me on this extraordinary journey of thanksgiving. Let us walk hand in hand, united by gratitude and purpose, destined for greatness. Together, we can live in harmony, embracing the transformational power of a thankful heart.

7. The Law of Unity

"Even the weak become strong when they are united". Friedrich von Schiller

"Make every effort to keep the unity of the Spirit through the bond of peace". Ephesians 4:3

Unity is the state of being joined as a whole, often marked by harmony, connection, and cooperation—with God, our inner selves, and others. During grief, expressing gratitude can foster a profound sense of unity, helping us feel connected to a greater whole. This connection brings deeper understanding and appreciation of our shared humanity and spiritual essence.

In times of sorrow, gratitude can be a powerful tool for experiencing unity with God. By recognising divine presence and guidance, even amidst pain, we find comfort and reassurance that transcend earthly struggles. Gratitude opens our hearts to the eternal love and compassion that sustain us through life's challenges, offering glimpses of peace and hope in difficult times.

"Come to me, all who labour and are heavy laden, and I will give you rest. Take my yoke upon you, and learn from me, for I am gentle and lowly in heart, and you will find rest for your souls. For my yoke is easy, and my burden is light". Matthew 11:28-30

"The Lord is near to the broken-hearted and saves the crushed in spirit". Psalm 34:18

Gratitude also strengthens our unity with ourselves. By acknowledging our inner strength, resilience, and wisdom, we come to appreciate our own beauty and grace. This self-compassion nurtures acceptance of our grief, allowing us to embrace our vulnerabilities with kindness and understanding. It transforms pain into self-awareness, helping us grow through even the most trying moments.

Furthermore, gratitude builds unity with others. Recognising the love, support, and kindness from family, friends, and strangers creates bonds of compassion and interconnectedness. This shared humanity provides solace and strength, reminding us that we are never alone in our grief. These connections create mutual understanding and care, offering healing as we navigate life's storms.

> *"Where there is unity there is always victory".*
> *Publilius Syrus*

By practising gratitude, we invite harmony and healing into our hearts. Gratitude becomes a sacred tool, helping us find solace, strength, and connection in life's most challenging moments. It turns grief into a source of resilience, allowing us to experience unity even in pain. It allows us to find light in darkness, meaning in loss, and appreciation for the love and support surrounding us. By embracing gratitude, we unlock its transformational power, creating a path toward healing, strength, and spiritual connection.

When I lost my mum, I came to understand that I had not truly lost her. My mum's spirit endures, having departed this world to reunite with God. Hence, why should I grieve for someone who is now united with my Creator? In being one with Him, I am also connected to my mum and dad—who are one with Him. Though no longer present in this physical world, they dwell in the presence of God and live in me. Their spirit is eternal. As spiritual beings, we are merely having a natural, physical experience during our time on earth—and our spirit lives on, long after we are gone.

Gratitude transforms grief into a bridge, connecting us with the divine, our inner selves, and the people around us. It reveals our divine essence and true nature—as spiritual beings—transcending the limitations of the physical body. Like a bridge, it helps us navigate the vast landscape of sorrow, fostering solidarity through our shared experiences of loss and healing.

Let gratitude guide us as we navigate the depths of grief, helping us uncover the beauty, love, and unity that lie within even the darkest moments.

8. The Law of Destiny

For I know the plans I have for you," declares the Lord, "plans to prosper you and not to harm you, plans to give you hope and a future. Jeremiah 29:11

"Today I have given you the choice between life and death, between blessings and curses. Now I call on heaven and earth to witness the

choice you make. Oh, that you would choose life, so that you and your descendants might live!" Deuteronomy 30:19

Destiny can be defined as the predetermined course of events or the ultimate outcome of one's life, often believed to be guided by fate, providence, or a higher power— God. It entails a purposeful direction towards a specific end or result. Destiny is believed to be beyond human control and influenced by a higher power or force. It encompasses the belief that certain events in our lives are meant to happen, leading us towards a specific outcome or path.

When we face the unfathomable depths of grief, expressing gratitude can serve as a profound lens through which we come to appreciate and acknowledge Divine Destiny. It allows us to see beyond the veil of sorrow and focus on the bigger picture of life, woven with purpose and meaning that goes beyond what we can fully understand. Instead of viewing our pain as a random and senseless occurrence, gratitude allows us to see the bigger picture, recognising that every twist and turn in our journey is a part of a greater design that is connected to the purpose and meaning of our lives.

When we lose a loved one or something dear to us, the practice of expressing gratitude serves as a poignant reminder of the preciousness of life and the transitory nature of our existence. We are reminded that each moment we share with our loved ones or the things we hold dear is a momentary yet beautiful reminder of the Divine Destiny that binds us all together.

Through the lens of gratitude, we come to honour the life of our loved ones or the things we have lost, not with tears of sorrow, but with hearts brimming with thankfulness for the gifts they have bestowed upon us. Their presence in our lives, no matter how short, reminds us of how Divine Destiny blends love, loss, and longing into the course of our lives.

Ultimately, the practice of expressing gratitude during grief allows us to find solace and healing in the embrace of Divine Destiny. It is through the lens of thankfulness that we come to see the beauty in the brokenness, the light in the darkness, and the purpose in the pain, forging a deeper connection to the profound mysteries that lie at the heart of our existence.

When we find ourselves overwhelmed by sorrow, expressing gratitude can become a transformative act, opening the door to a profound connection with God and his Divine Plan. Gratitude serves as a bridge, linking our earthly experiences with the unseen forces that shape our lives, offering glimpses of a deeper meaning and purpose.

As we navigate through our loss, gratitude becomes our steady guide, quietly teaching us to honour the memories of those we have loved or the things we have lost—not with bitterness, but with hearts full of appreciation for the joy and lessons they brought into our lives. It reminds us that even in absence, their presence continues to shine through us and shape us.

Expressing gratitude in grief is like planting seeds of hope in barren soil, watering them with tears of remembrance until they bloom into flowers of healing and acceptance. It allows us to confront our pain with a thankful heart, seeing not only the wounds of loss but also the strength and growth that emerge from our struggles.

It unveils the resilience of the human spirit. In these moments of vulnerability, we are reminded of the strength and beauty within us, inviting us to embrace the mystery of Divine Destiny with trust and open hearts.

> *"Hardships often prepare ordinary people for an extraordinary destiny". C.S. Lewis.*

I take this opportunity to share with you a powerful and true story of redemption and destiny. The journey of Mary Johnson and Oshea Israel is a profound example of forgiveness, transformation, and the enduring power of love and destiny. Their story, which began with tragedy, evolved into an extraordinary testimony of reconciliation, healing, and destiny.

In 1993, Mary Johnson's 20-year-old son, Laramiun Byrd, was tragically shot during an altercation at a party in Minneapolis, Minnesota. The perpetrator, Oshea Israel, was just 16 years old. Convicted of second-degree murder, Oshea was sentenced to 25½ years in prison. For Mary, the loss of her only child was devastating, and her grief soon turned into anger and bitterness towards the young man responsible.

Mary shared her grief and inner struggle in her own words:

"Three days later, I was told they'd picked up the 16-year-old boy who had taken Laramiun's life. I believe hate set in then and there. Here I was, a Christian woman, full of hatred.

I was pleased he was going to be tried as an adult for first-degree murder, so when the judge suddenly reduced the charge to second-degree murder, I was furious. In court, I viewed Oshea as an animal, and the only thing that kept me going was the opportunity to give my victim impact statement. Inspired by my faith, I ended by saying I'd forgiven Oshea 'because the Bible tells us to forgive.' When Oshea's mother gave her statement and asked us to forgive him, I thought I had.

But the truth was, I hadn't forgiven him. The root of bitterness ran deep; anger had taken hold, and I hated everyone. I remained like this for years, pushing many people away. Then one day, I came across a poem that spoke of two mothers—one whose child had been murdered and the other whose child was the murderer.

It was such a healing poem all about the commonality of pain and it revealed to me my destiny. Suddenly I had this vision of creating an organisation to support not only the mothers of murdered children but also the mothers of children who had taken a life. I knew then that I would never be able to deal with these mothers if I hadn't really forgiven Oshea. So I put in a request to the Department of Corrections to meet him."

Mary, inspired by her faith, recognised that forgiveness was her only path to healing. In 2005, she took the brave step of meeting Oshea, who was still in prison. Their initial meeting, arranged through a restorative justice programme, was deeply emotional. Mary confronted Oshea with the pain he had caused but expressed her desire to forgive him.

For Oshea, the encounter was life-changing. He had carried the weight of guilt and remorse for years, and Mary's act of forgiveness gave him an opportunity to reflect and seek redemption. Over time, their relationship grew from forgiveness into an unlikely yet profound friendship. Oshea came to see Mary not only as a mentor but as a mother figure.

When Oshea was released from prison in 2010, Mary did something extraordinary: she welcomed him into her community and helped him reintegrate into society. Their bond deepened, and Oshea often referred to Mary as "Mum." Together, they began sharing their story at schools, churches, and community events, advocating for forgiveness, restorative justice, and healing.

Mary reflected on her meeting with Oshea and her journey towards healing:

"Having never been to a prison before, I was terrified when we arrived and wanted to turn back. But when Oshea came into the room I shook hands with him and said, 'I don't know you and you don't know me. You didn't know my son and he didn't know you, so we need to lay down a foundation and get to know one another.' We talked for two hours, during which he admitted what he'd done. I could see how sorry he was. At the end of the meeting, for the very first time, I was genuinely able to say that I forgave Oshea. He couldn't believe I could do this and asked if he could hug me. When he left the room, I bent over, saying, 'I've just hugged the man who murdered my son.' Then, as I stood up, I felt something rising from the soles of my feet and leaving me. From that day on, I haven't felt any hatred, animosity, or anger. It was over.

In March 2010, we held a welcome home party for Oshea, organised by my organisation and some Catholic nuns from the neighbourhood. Even ex-gang members from Chicago came to witness what was happening. When Oshea told me he wanted to share our story publicly to help others, I was amazed by his courage. He is my spiritual son. It's not always easy for us to stand together, time and again, and recount our story. But I tell other mothers that talking and sharing your story is the road to healing."

This remarkable journey reminds us that embracing forgiveness and destiny enables us to walk through grief with faith and grace. It offers comfort in the belief that even the most painful experiences are part of a greater, meaningful design. By accepting this, we can find restoration, hope, and a deeper understanding of life's purpose.

9. The Law of Enlightenment

"I pray that the eyes of your heart may be enlightened in order that you may know the hope to which he has called you" Ephesians 1:18

Now, let us uncover the supreme law and transformational power gratitude entrapped in the final E in GRATITUDE— enlightenment.

Enlightenment is a state of profound spiritual understanding or insight, often associated with the awakening of higher consciousness, wisdom, and awareness. It involves a deep sense of clarity, peace, and liberation from the limitations of the ego or the material world, leading to a state of spiritual transcendence and unity with the Divine.

> *"Then you will know the truth, and the truth will set you free."*
> John 8:32

Expressing gratitude in times of grief can become a transformative force, leading us towards spiritual enlightenment and healing. When we choose gratitude amidst sorrow and pain, we unlock the hidden beauty, lessons, and blessings that even the darkest moments of our lives can offer. Gratitude becomes a guiding light, illuminating the interconnectedness of all things and revealing the goodness that exists within the universe.

In the absurdity of grief and gratitude, we discover that by recognising and valuing the love, memories, and support surrounding us during times of loss, we can rise above our pain and suffering. Gratitude allows us to honour the past, treasure the present, and embrace the future with renewed purpose and grace. Just as a seed must first rest in darkness before it can sprout into life, so too must we accept grief with a spirit of gratitude, enabling the growth and transformation that leads to spiritual awakening.

Like a phoenix rising from the ashes, our journey through grief, when guided by gratitude, can elevate us to a higher spiritual plane where strength, resilience, and inner peace are revealed. Surrendering to God and opening our hearts to gratitude helps us release the burdens of sorrow and fear, allowing our spirits to ascend towards healing and enlightenment. Much like the lotus flower blooming in murky waters, gratitude amid grief allows the soul to blossom, symbolising the beauty and resilience that emerge from pain and loss.

Gratitude in grief does not deny or dismiss our emotions and pain. Instead, it honours them with appreciation and reverence. Through the interchange of gratitude and grief, we transform pain into wisdom, sorrow into compassion, and loss into a deeper connection with ourselves, God, and the world around us. It is in this sacred union of gratitude and surrender that we experience spiritual transformation, paving the way for healing, growth, and profound peace.

As we practise gratitude during grief, we begin to see how even the smallest acts of love, comfort, and support can ripple through us, creating waves of healing and transformation. Gratitude nurtures resilience, acceptance, and hope, guiding us from the shadows of despair into the light of spiritual enlightenment.

Just as a candle shines brightest in darkness, our gratitude during grief lights the path towards healing and growth. By focusing on what we still hold dear, we shift our perspective from loss and despair to hope and renewal. Gratitude taps into a deep reservoir of inner strength and grace, enabling us to confront our pain, learn from our experiences, and extend compassion to ourselves and others.

In the process of overcoming grief, it becomes evident that the more we cherish the love and memories of those we've lost, the more we open ourselves to healing and comfort. Gratitude fosters a sense of reciprocity, bringing solace to sorrow, connection to isolation, and peace to turmoil. It allows us to become more resilient, leading us to a profound understanding and acceptance of life's transitions.

Ultimately, the expression of gratitude during grief serves as a sacred bridge between our pain and our healing, our loss and our growth, our despair and our enlightenment. It is in the act of embracing gratitude that we honour the complexity of our emotions, the depth of our connections, and the beauty of our shared humanity. Through the lens of gratitude, we are able to see beyond the veil of suffering and loss, towards a horizon of hope, renewal, and spiritual awakening.

In conclusion, the supreme law of gratitude offers us a profound opportunity to elevate our spirits, deepen our connections, and transcend our grief towards a higher spiritual path of healing and enlightenment. By embracing gratitude in the face of grief, we open ourselves up to a transformative journey of self-discovery, resilience, and grace, allowing us to find solace, meaning, and purpose in the midst of our pain. It is through the power of gratitude that we can truly experience the transformational power of healing and enlightenment, leading us towards a greater sense of peace, wholeness, and connection with God, ourselves, and the world around us.

Enlightenment is the profound realisation of who you truly are—a spiritual being, elevated and seated with God, united with your divine purpose. In this state of unity, there is no fear, no loss, no lack, and no longing, for you are whole and complete. It is a place where the divine essence within you aligns seamlessly with the Creator, offering clarity, peace, and fulfilment.

How complete do you feel? How connected to your true essence? I invite you to join me in gratitude, stepping boldly into the unity that transforms and elevates.

The spirit within you is life itself—your breath, your being. When the breath of life departs from the body, as it did for my mum and dad, the physical form ceases, but the spirit remains eternal. True life is not in the physical; it is in the spirit, which is untethered by worldly constraints, limitless and abundant.

Walking in unity with God allows the spirit to lead, to rise to its fullest potential. In this unity, you recognise every gift and talent He has entrusted to you, equipping you to fulfil your unique purpose on Earth. You are one with Him, and through this oneness, you discover the depth of His love, the boundlessness of His grace, and the magnitude of the calling He has placed upon your life.

I hereby call on you to step into gratitude, embrace your divine essence, and live as the spiritual being you are, fully alive, enlightened, and elevated, walking in the completeness of His presence.

As we conclude this journey, let us commit to practising gratitude daily and embracing the supreme laws of gratitude in our lives. By doing so, we unlock its transformative potential and full splendour, allowing us to heal, conquer grief, and cultivate a life of profound joy and peace.

I invite you to take a moment each day to reflect on the blessings, both big and small, that fill your life. Ask yourself: what can I be grateful for today that money cannot purchase, no matter how challenging the circumstances? Embrace the power of gratitude as a tool for healing by consciously shifting your focus from loss to appreciation, from darkness to light.

Recognise that even in moments of pain, there is always something to be thankful for, something that can empower you to rise above your struggles. Let gratitude guide your thoughts, words, and actions, and allow its power to reshape your perspective, heal your heart, and restore your soul. Step into each day with a heart full of thankfulness, and watch as the world around you transforms in ways you never thought possible.

I would love to conclude with this profound hymn, "*What a Friend We Have in Jesus*". This Christian hymn was originally written as a poem in 1855 by preacher Joseph M. Scriven to comfort his mother, who was living in Ireland while he was in Canada.

I encourage you to play this song if you can, sing along with the lyrics, or simply listen and reflect.

Be richly blessed and surrender your pain and burdens as you read, sing, or listen to the song:

What a friend we have in Jesus
All our sins and griefs to bear
What a privilege to carry
Everything to God in prayer

O what peace we often forfeit
O what needless pain we bear
All because we do not carry
Everything to God in prayer

Have we trials and temptations?
Is there trouble anywhere?
We should never be discouraged
Take it to the Lord in prayer

Can we find a friend so faithful
Who will all our sorrows share?
Jesus knows our every weakness
Take it to the Lord in prayer

With immense love and gratitude,
Dr Sylvia Forchap-Likambi.

References

1. Zahn, R., Garrido, G., Moll, J., & Grafman, J. (2007). *Individual differences in posterior cortical volume and reward valuation: Evidence from gratitude trait effects on the brain.* NeuroImage, 34(1), 1-10.

2. Emmons, R. A., & McCullough, M. E. (2003). *Counting blessings versus burdens: An experimental investigation of gratitude and subjective well-being in daily life.* Journal of Personality and Social Psychology, 84(2), 377–389.

3. Wong, Y. J., Owen, J., Gabana, N. T., Brown, J. W., McInnis, S., Toth, P., & Gilman, L. (2018). *Does gratitude writing improve the mental health of psychotherapy clients? Evidence from a randomized controlled trial.* Psychotherapy Research, 28(2), 192–202.

4. Emmons, R. A., & McCullough, M. E. (2003). Counting blessings versus burdens: An experimental investigation of gratitude and subjective well-being in daily life. Psychological Science, 14(6), 426–430.

5. Calhoun, L. G., & Tedeschi, R. G. (2006). Handbook of posttraumatic growth: Research and practice. Lawrence Erlbaum Associates.

6. Maltby, J., Day, L., & Macaskill, A. (2006). The role of gratitude in the development of positive psychology. The Journal of Positive Psychology, 1(2), 58–65.

7. Kashdan, T. B., Mishra, A., Breen, W. E., & Froh, J. J. (2009). Gender differences in gratitude: Examining appraisals, narratives, the willingness to express emotions, and changes in subjective well-being. *Personality and Individual Differences*, 47(8), 888-893.

About the Author
Dr Sylvia Forchap-Likambi

Dr. Sylvia Forchap-Likambi is a visionary, multi-award-winning leading empowerment and transformation authority, transformational Speaker/ Coach, and seven-times international best-selling author; specialized in the delivery of very high quality/cutting-edge empowerment and revolutionary leadership and transformation programs. She is the Founder and Global Chair of The Global Visionary Women Network, Founder and CEO of "Behaviour Changed" Award Winning Community Interest Company, Voice of Nations; and Global CEO/Consultant of Dr Sylvia Likambi International/ Dr Sylvia Likambi International Health & Wellbeing Clinic.

Over the years, she has coached, empowered, inspired, and positively impacted/ transformed over 1.5 million lives globally, thousands of female entrepreneurs, and relentlessly empowered many to come out of addictions, depression, get into training, volunteering, employment/self-employment, leadership roles; and also offered them several of such opportunities through her organizations.

She grew up in Cameroon, and later moved to Italy where she earned a Doctor of Pharmacy degree and a PhD degree. She was awarded the Italian Ministry of Higher Education and Research scholarship for excellence, and the Australian- Europe Scholarships to accomplish a year's collaboration with the University of Sydney (Nepean Hospital). At completion of her PhD in Australia and Italy, she worked as Postdoctoral Researcher in Italy and the UK; and became Honorary Research Associate with the Royal Liverpool University Hospital in 2008, and a member of The European Hematology Association in 2009.

Dr Sylvia has participated immensely in leukaemia research and is author/co-author in a number of international peer reviewed journals. She is also an ILM certified executive and business/Life Coach and a bestselling author. She was nominated in the African Business Chamber's UK TOP 100 African Business Leaders and Entrepreneurs 2022 and 2024 Lists, and listed on the Top 25 Black Entrepreneurs To Watch in 2021 by The UK Black Business Show. She was also the winner of Honorary Award for Exemplary Professional Leadership Recognition at the Enterprise Minds Awards 2018, The Positive Role Model for Gender Award at The UK National Diversity Awards 2016, and multiple nominee/ finalist for

Mentoring Champion of the Year at The SEN Powerful Together Awards 2012-2014, and The Member's Choice Awards in 2012 and 2013 (which celebrates the achievements of an individual who can demonstrate their commitment and contribution to the world of social enterprise, and critically, how they have enabled entrepreneurs to achieve their goals and aspirations).

She brings a very unique and dynamic blend of inspiration, purpose, empowerment, and transformation in her mentoring, coaching, and engagements; that has the potential of transforming the most dormant/negative mindset into a highly productive/positive and dynamic mindset, capable of setting and achieving any life goal.

She is a strong believer of the fact that as leaders we are called to serve rather than being served, and that to whom much is given much is expected. As a result, she endlessly embarks on a selfless journey of service and giving back to her community without an expectation of being financially rewarded or praised. Her greatest reward is in the satisfaction she gets from experiencing lives being transformed as a result of her humble service to humanity.

Her ethnicity, life experiences, educational background, resilient nature, and down to earth personality has given her the tremendous opportunity and privilege to serve and interact with some of the most deprived and underprivileged within diverse cultures, educational backgrounds, and communities; inspiring and challenging them to step forth confidently to unleash their untapped potentials and fulfil their dreams, regardless of their background, gender or circumstances.

She has also delivered several successful and life transforming revolutionary leadership, empowerment programs for VON (leading it to earn the prestigious SEN Behaviour Changed Award in 2013), WEA, and a host of commissioned projects nationally and internationally.

Dr Sylvia's life is true testament of her authority and leadership; she's a power wife and power mum to three incredibly gifted and talented children who are some of the world's and our nation's youngest authors of multiple books.

She has featured on several national and international Radio and TV stations, to speak on the theme of female empowerment, entrepreneurship, leadership, and other topics; and been guest/keynote speaker to several audiences, ranging from community groups to universities.

About the Publisher

Likambi Global Publishing Ltd
Email: enquiries@likambiglobalpublishing.com
Tel: +44 (0) 7539 216072
www.likambiglobalpublishing.com

We are a Dynamic Family-Led Cutting-Edge Global Publisher set up to simplify and enhance your writing and publishing experience and unique journey to becoming a renowned and confident author.

Whether you are an adult or child, we have a special team that is devoted to working with you throughout your writing and publishing journey with us! All of our consultants and coaches/mentors are bestselling authors with years of hands-on experience and a wealth of knowledge uniquely tailored to meet your individual needs!

Our goal is to provide you with the ultimate writing and publishing experience required to share your unique message and voice as an author with the world and strive to greater heights!

Publications are done three times a year; January, June, and November. All manuscripts must be received at least 90 days prior to publication dates.

www.ingramcontent.com/pod-product-compliance
Lightning Source LLC
Chambersburg PA
CBHW041144110526
44590CB00027B/4118